complete patio book

Consulting Editor: Don Vandervort

Staff for this Book:

Senior Editor: Jim McRae

Art Director: Odette Sévigny

Editor: Rob Lutes

Assistant Editors: Ned Meredith, Jennifer Ormston

Researcher: Adam van Sertima

Designers: Jean-Guy Doiron, Robert Labelle

Picture Editor: Jennifer Meltzer

Photographer: Robert Chartier

Production Coordinator: Dominique Gagné

Systems Director: Edward Renaud

Scanner Operators: Martin Francoeur, Sara Grynspan

Technical Support: Jean Sirois

Proofreader: Judy Yelon

Indexer: Linda Cardella Cournoyer

Book Consultant:

Richard Day

The *Complete Patio Book* was produced in conjunction with
ST. REMY MULTIMEDIA

Cover:

Photography: Phil Harvey

Photo Director: JoAnn Masaoka Van Atta

Landscape Architect: Louis Morano

Landscape Contractors: Martin Ragno and Associates

VP, Editorial Director, Sunset Books: Bob Doyle

90 QPD/QPD 9 8 7 6 5 4 3

ISBN 0-376-01397-4
Library of Congress Catalog Card Number: 97-80056
Printed in the United States

For additional copies of the *Complete Patio Book,* or any other
Sunset book, call 1-800-526-5111, or visit our
website at www.sunsetbooks.com

complete patio book

Sunset

Table of Contents

A Gallery
OF HOME
PATIOS

Warm weather beckons us outdoors, to dine with friends, to read a good book, or just to relax and enjoy the sunshine. What better place for these leisure activities than the patio, with its smoothly paved surface, surrounding plants, and comfortable furniture? Think of a patio as a bridge between the house and the garden—a transition zone that brings you closer to the outdoors.

As an extension of your home, a patio can offer you all the comforts of indoor living; as part of the garden, perhaps even detached from the house, it can become a favorite lounging and entertaining area. No matter what your climate, you can shape your patio into an attractive outdoor room you will enjoy as long as the weather will allow—overheads, strategically placed fences, and sheltering shrubs and trees can extend your patio season or make midday meals more comfortable. Over the following pages, you'll see some of the countless ways people have adapted their patios for outdoor living, and gain a wealth of ideas for creating an outdoor room that's right for you.

Shaded by mature trees, this concrete-paver patio is an island of calm in a busy world, a perfect place to while away the hours on a weekend afternoon.

Sleek stone steps join the two levels of this backyard patio, which echoes the two-tiered roof above. Potted plants provide a sense of enclosure and bring garden greenery up close.

Terra-cotta tiles, a low stuccoed wall and luxuriant plants evoke a classic feel in this cozy patio nook.

A river runs through it—or seems to. Highlighted by dark blue tiles and randomly spaced islands, the cool blue curves of this "river" will never overrun their concrete banks. Divider walls in solid colors provide privacy and warm contrast. *Landscape architect: Delaney & Cochran.*

Concrete pavers, made to look like stone cobbles, and a freestanding metal trellis bring an old-world charm to this patio retreat.

Washed river stones and randomly shaped flagstones stud this concrete patio, which encompasses both arid and wet landscapes. A water feature such as this one is especially welcome in a dry climate.

Raised planting beds on three sides and the house wall on the other give the tile patio above its intimate appeal. Potted plants provide islands of color.

Gravel, retained by peeled-log risers, makes a simple walkway in a gently sloping garden with Japanese influences *(right)*.

On a multilevel flagstone
patio, steps lead from
a house-shaded section
to a lower-level landing.
The hillside property is
contained by a flagstone
retaining wall that doubles
as steps and ties all the
elements together.
*Landscape architect:
Katzmaier, Newell, Kehr.*

The austere look of a seeded aggregate patio and concrete retaining wall is balanced by a colorful bank of flowers and towering trees. *Landscape architect: R. David Adams Associates.*

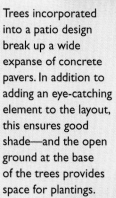

Trees incorporated into a patio design break up a wide expanse of concrete pavers. In addition to adding an eye-catching element to the layout, this ensures good shade—and the open ground at the base of the trees provides space for plantings.

A stone retaining wall is used to reclaim a steep-sided backyard, creating room for a secluded dining area. The terraced garden surrounds the space with color and life.

Ample counter space and built-in grill make outdoor cooking a pleasure here. The patio overhead ensures barbecues are never rained out.

In a carefully ordered landscape design, a narrow, urban lot is transformed into a beautiful garden hideaway. A tall hedge offers shelter, privacy, and insulation from the sounds of the city. *Design: Chris Jackson.*

Seeded aggregate paving and brick dividers are combined in a formal entry courtyard. The brick motif is repeated in the curving trim of the wall fountain. *Landscape architect: Robert Chittock.*

At the entrance to an early Californian rancho-style house, vine-covered timbers and flagstone patio create a transition zone—or *corredor*—between indoors and out. The roof provides partial shade and lets in the rain, helping to keep the house cool.

A winding fieldstone wall encloses a broad patio. The stones of the wall were applied with mortar over a base of concrete blocks.
Landscape contractor: Bertotti Landscaping, Inc.

With a lush forest backdrop, a spa and lap pool are the focal point of the mortared-brick patio below. Contrasting brick patterns are set off by precise white grout lines.

Planning
YOUR PATIO

*Planning is the essential first step to any successful patio.
Even if you already have a good idea of the basic patio style you
want, you need to take the time to consider carefully where you
want to locate it, and then go one step further by putting your ideas
down on paper. This chapter offers an in-depth look at basic
design considerations and explains some of the site factors that
will determine where you put your patio—sun, wind, rain, snow,
and microclimates. Next comes the hands-on design process—from
drawing a basic map of your property, through sketching and
experimenting to polishing up your final plan. You'll need this
plan whether you hire a professional or carry out the work
yourself. Along the way we'll discuss general design guidelines,
provide you with all the information you'll need to deal with
building codes and variances, and give you some tips for hiring
pros. Do you need specific examples for inspiration? Turn to
pages 46 to 49 to see the makeovers that several landscape
architects and designers planned for two typical lots.*

An overhanging tree transforms this cozy patio
made from interlocking bricks into a personal
sanctuary. Flowers and surrounding trees add
to an atmosphere of quiet relaxation.

A Patio Primer

The first step in planning your patio is to focus clearly on your family's needs and habits. Think about the way you spend your leisure time.

GETTING STARTED

Consider your lifestyle. Do you entertain frequently outdoors? If so, do you prefer casual or formal entertaining? How much time do you want to spend gardening and maintaining your yard? Do you have pets that might damage frag-ile patio plants and furniture? Your answers to these questions will determine some basic design elements for your patio.

Next, evaluate the assets and liabilities of your yard. Even if you plan to enlist the services of a landscape architect or other pro-fessional *(page 44)*, you need to have a good understanding of your existing landscape.

Can your patio capitalize on a beautiful view? Is your property bounded by woods? Perhaps your design can take advantage of a sunny southern exposure, mature plantings, or focus on one element, such as an attractive tree.

Consider also your yard's poten-tial handicaps. Is your lot on a steep slope? How much of the lot is exposed to street traffic and noise? Is humidity a problem in your area during the summer months? Does your present patio open off the wrong room, get too much sun or shade, or lack suffi-cient space? You'll want to plan a

A circle of flagstone pavers, set off by dramatic, vine-draped columns, makes an intimate dining area. The design of the overhead is echoed by the gate in the background.

patio that minimizes your yard's special problems.

The exact location of your patio will depend largely on the size and contour of your lot, the way your house sits on it, the uses you have in mind for your patio, and your climate. A number of different site possibilities and configurations are shown on pages 29 to 33 and in the first chapter.

SUCCESSFUL PATIO DESIGN

Regardless of the size of your lot and any landscaping problems your property may present, suc-cessful patio design depends to a large extent upon the following five key elements:

Flexibility: Your design needs to accommodate the various activi-ties important to your family.

Privacy: As an extension of your indoor space, your patio should offer a similar feeling of privacy.

Comfort: You'll be most comfort-able on a patio designed to accom-modate your area's climate and your property's microclimate.

Safety: Patio paving materials have different properties. For example, some become slippery when wet, others are too sharp or uneven if you have children or for playing games. Consider the traffic patterns from house to patio and from garden to patio. They need to be safe, with adequate lighting provided at any steps and along garden paths.

Beauty: Successful patios achieve a certain balance in an overall garden scheme. Materials used in patio construction should blend with those in the house; colors and textures should harmonize with the landscaping and other decorative accents.

Garden flowers provide an attractive border to this cut-sandstone patio and contrast with the surrounding forest. The high fence and arbor further define the area.

SETTING A STYLE

The first decision you must make is whether you want a formal or informal patio environment.

Formal landscapes are typically symmetrical, with straight lines, geometric patterns, and near perfect balance; they often include neatly sheared hedges, topiaries, and a fountain, pool, or sculpture, and are always closely maintained.

Small rectangular plots are well suited to the medieval knot-garden style, with brick or stone pathways and formal plantings radiating from a central fountain or sculpture. By replacing the brick or stone with adobe and tile, the style becomes Spanish.

Concrete lends a slightly industrial look to a formal patio garden. Seeded aggregate, smooth-troweled and textured concrete are modern in feel.

Elegant wrought-iron furniture brings a formal touch to a simple stone patio. Potted plants and sundial add a sense of order, while the raised flower bed breaks up the surrounding area.

This striking patio design is full of surprises and visual appeal. The vibrant color of the concrete paving works well with the generally earthy colors of the house.

Informal styles, on the other hand, tend toward curves, asymmetry and apparent randomness. These patios are often easier to maintain. Adjacent plantings are usually more informal as well.

Contemporary designs might feature such things as multilevel surfaces, planters, overheads, or a swimming pool, and low-maintenance plantings. Irregular flagstone or mossy bricks laid in the sand offer a softer cottage-garden look, as do spaced concrete pavers, especially if you plant ground cover between the units.

Raked gravel that imitates swirling water, carefully placed boulders, a spill fountain, and a hidden garden bench or bridge are all trademarks of a Japanese garden.

In desert climates, the patio can function as a retreat from heat and noise; overheads and screens, a fountain or a waterfall, and lush plants with drip lines or spray emitters can be incorporated into the design to keep the air cool and moist.

FOUR LANDSCAPING PRINCIPLES

Whatever landscape style you choose, observing the four basic landscaping principles will ensure that your patio is a pleasure to behold. Good landscaping professionals, through years of experience, have absorbed these guidelines so well that they never lose sight of them during the design process.

It's a good idea to return to this section repeatedly as your plan develops. When your design is complete, check back to make sure that you haven't forgotten or altered your original intentions amid the flurry of last-minute planning considerations.

Unity: Unity means that everything in your patio looks like it belongs together—paving, overhead, and screens complement each other, furniture suits the patio's architectural style, and the patio's plants relate to each other and to the other plants in the garden.

Unity between patio and house is an important consideration, too. For example, if your patio is built off a kitchen that is decorated in a casual style, the patio should have the same feeling.

Variety: Variety keeps unity from becoming monotonous. A good design offers an element of surprise: a path that leads from a large main terrace to a more intimate one; a plant display that brings the garden into the patio; a subtle wall fountain that gives dimension to a small space; trees that provide varying degrees of light at different times of day.

You can make use of variety on vertical planes, too. Patios at different levels, low walls, raised beds, privacy screens, and container plants of varying heights help draw the eye away from a vertical expanse.

Proportion: Proportion demands that your patio structure be in scale with your house and garden. Keep in mind that as an outdoor room, patios are built on a different scale than indoor rooms. Though many patios are scaled to the size of the living room, don't be afraid to design something larger. Outdoor furniture usually takes up more room than indoor pieces, and you may want room for containers of plants. Choose plants with their ultimate size in mind.

There are sensible limits, however. If your lot is so big that you need a large patio to keep everything in scale, try to create a few smaller areas within the larger whole. For example, squares of plantings inset in paving will break up a monotonous surface. Baffle plantings or fences can divide one large area into one or more functional spaces.

To maintain proportion in a small patio, keep the design simple and uncluttered. Clean lines make the elements seem larger. Stepped planting beds lead the eye up and out of a confined area. Tall vertical screens used to enclose a small area actually make it appear larger, as does such solid paving as brick, with its small-scale repetitive pattern.

This small island of cobblestones provides a good vantage point to enjoy the view of the water or watch a game of croquet. Hardy teak furniture stands up to nasty weather. Chairs, table, and container plants can be repositioned, allowing maximum flexibility.

Balance: Balance is achieved when elements are artfully combined to produce the same visual weight (*not* symmetry) on either side of a center of interest. For example, if your patio is shaded on one side by a mature tree, you can balance the tree's weight with perimeter benches on the other side.

A mortared-brick surface adds warmth to a formal patio. The low wall defines the space and provides a platform for potted ferns.

Trellis walls and an overhead thick with vines combine to produce a perfect retreat for a hot day. Identical plants on either side of the patio provide balance.

Understanding Weather

Knowing your climate is essential to planning a patio. If you know what to expect from the weather around you, you can plan a patio that will be enjoyable over the longest possible season, and one that will take advantage of the weather tendencies of your property.

If you've lived in your present home for a number of seasons, you're already familiar with your climate's benefits and hazards. But if you're new to the area, you may want to obtain accurate information to help you get acquainted with general weather patterns. Such information is available from local U.S. weather bureau offices, public power or utility companies, meteorology departments on college and university campuses, and county agricultural extension offices.

YOUR RELATION TO THE SUN

A patio's exposure to the sun is one of the most important factors in your enjoyment of the space. Knowing the sun's path over your prop-erty may prompt you to adjust the site of your proposed patio, extend its dimensions, or change its design in order to add a few weeks or months of sun or shade to your outdoor room. Often you can moderate the effects of the sun with the addition of a patio roof.

Basic orientation: Theoretically, a patio that faces north is cold because it rarely receives the sun. A south-facing patio is usually warm because, from sunrise to sunset, the sun never leaves it. A patio

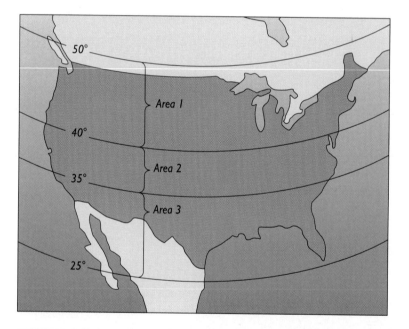

SUN AND SHADE

Sun and shade are cast at various angles, depending on the time of year and where you live. Find your location on the map at left; then refer to the chart below for the sun angles and hours of daylight on your property.

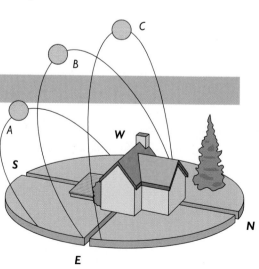

THE SUN IN YOUR YARD			
SEASONAL SUN ANGLES	**SUN'S POSITION/HOURS OF DAYLIGHT (SEE MAP ABOVE)**		
Season (date)	Area 1	Area 2	Area 3
A) Noon, 12/21	21°/8 hrs.	29°/9 hrs.	37°/10 hrs.
B) Noon, 3/21 & 9/21	45°/12 hrs.	53°/12 hrs.	60°/12 hrs.
C) Noon, 6/21	69°/16 hrs.	76°/15 hrs.	83°/14 hrs.

A tall fence provides shelter from prevailing winds, while leaving the patio open to the warm rays of the sun. Trees and vines have recently been planted to soften the look of the fence.

on the east side is cool, receiving only morning sun. And a patio that faces west is often unbearably hot because it receives the full force of the sun's midafternoon rays. In addition, late afternoon sun often creates a harsh glare.

Generally, your patio temperature will follow this north-south-east-west rule. Exceptions do occur in climates where extreme summer or winter temperatures are predictable. For example, the mid-July temperatures in Phoenix, Arizona, regularly climb above 100°, and a north-facing patio there could hardly be considered cold. But in San Francisco, on the other hand, a patio with a southern or western exposure could hardly be considered hot because chilly fogs and stiff ocean breezes are common during the summer months.

Seasonal path of the sun: Another factor to consider is the sun's path during the year (see drawing on facing page). As the sun passes over your house, it makes an arc that changes slightly every day, becoming higher in summer and lower in winter. Changes in the sun's path give us longer days in summer and shorter days in winter, and they also alter sun and shade patterns on your patio. Find your location on the map and then refer to the accompanying chart for sun angles and hours of daylight your property will receive.

BATTLING WIND, RAIN, AND SNOW

Like sun, wind can be a major foe—or ally—affecting patio comfort and enjoyment. Rain and snow, though admittedly more foreboding, can also be neutralized to some degree by careful planning.

Understanding wind: Study the wind patterns around your house and over your lot. Too much wind blowing across your patio on a cool day can be just as unpleasant as no breeze at all on a hot day. Evaluating the wind patterns will help you discover how to control it or encourage it with fences, screens, or plants.

Three different kinds of winds can affect your site: annual prevailing winds, localized seasonal breezes (daily, late afternoon, or summer), and occasional high-velocity winds generated by stormy weather.

Although you can determine the prevailing winds in your neighbor-

WIND DIRECTION/FENCE HEIGHT

Wind control studies indicate that a solid vertical screen or fence isn't necessarily the best barrier against the wind. Lattice *(facing page)* or spaced-wood screening provides diffused protection near fence. Fence-top baffle aimed into the wind offers the most shelter.

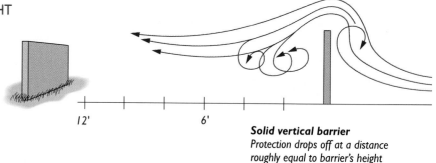

Solid vertical barrier
Protection drops off at a distance roughly equal to barrier's height

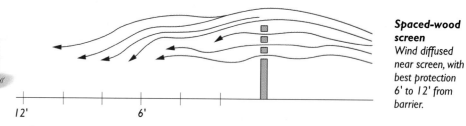

Spaced-wood screen
Wind diffused near screen, with best protection 6' to 12' from barrier.

Solid barrier, baffle angled toward patio
Best protection up to 8' from barrier.

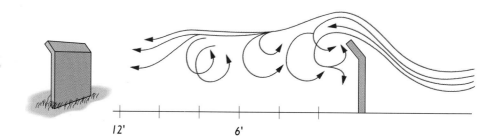

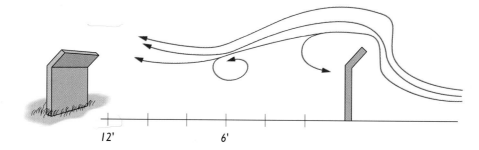

Solid barrier, baffle angled into the wind
Good protection near the barrier and to a distance of more than twice the barrier's height.

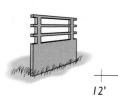

DEALING WITH WIND

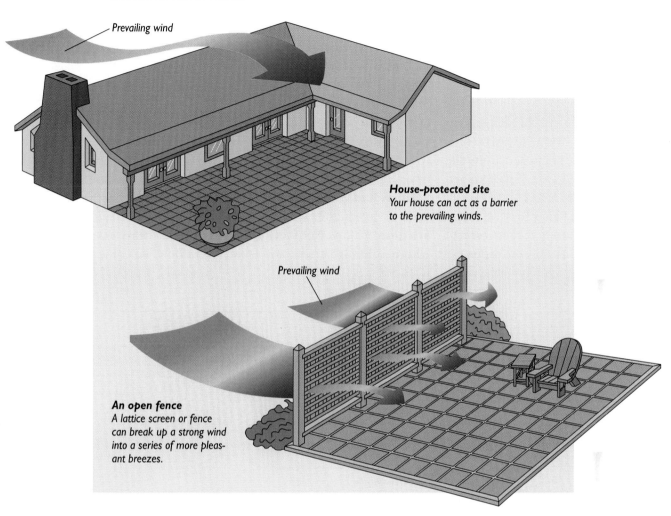

Prevailing wind

House-protected site
Your house can act as a barrier to the prevailing winds.

Prevailing wind

An open fence
A lattice screen or fence can break up a strong wind into a series of more pleasant breezes.

hood by noticing the direction the trees lean, chances are that the prevailing winds around your home are different. Wind flows like water, spilling over obstacles, breaking into currents, eddying and twisting. After blowing through the trees, the wind may spill over your house and drop onto your patio. If you're considering building a screen or fence to block wind from blowing across your patio, note that different wind barriers create different effects, as shown in the illustrations on the facing page. As they indicate, solid

barriers aren't necessarily the most effective ones.

To determine the screen or fence that's best suited to your situation, pinpoint the wind currents in your yard. Post small flags where you want wind protection and note their movement during windy periods.
Dealing with rain and snow: If, in assessing your climate, you learn that winter storms usually blow out of the northeast, you may want to locate your patio where it will take less of a beating from the weather—perhaps on the south side of the

house where it will be partially protected by trees or a roof overhang.

If you live in an area frequented by brief summer cloudbursts, you can extend the patio's usefulness with a solid roof *(page 91)* that lets you sit outdoors during the warm weather rains. Since it's easiest to lay the foundation for the roof at the same time that you build the patio, advance planning is a must. If you're located in snow country, be sure whatever overhead design you choose can handle snow and ice buildup.

YOUR PROPERTY'S MICROCLIMATE

Few people experience exactly the same temperature as the weather bureau. A reported temperature of 68° means that a thermometer in the shade, protected from the wind, reads 68°. If there's a 10 to 15 mile-per-hour breeze, a person in the shade will feel that the temperature is about 62°, while someone on a sunny patio sheltered from the breeze will experience a comfortable 75° to 78°.

This is an illustration of microclimates—pockets that are created by combinations of sun, exposure, and other factors. Though sun and wind are major factors, they're not the only ones. Several potential microclimates are shown in the drawings below.

Remember that cold air flows downhill like water, "puddles" in basins, and can also be dammed up by walls or solid fences. If you build a sunken patio or one that is walled in by your house and a retaining wall below house level, you may find yourself shivering at sunset while higher surroundings are quite balmy. Note any spots where cold air settles and frost is heavy.

Keep in mind, too, that certain materials reflect sun and/or heat better than others. For example, light-colored masonry paving and walls are great at spreading sun and heat, but they can be uncomfortably bright. Wood surfaces are usually cooler. On the other hand, dark masonry materials retain heat a little longer, making evening on your patio a little warmer. Plants help block the wind, but they let breezes through. Well-placed deciduous trees can shelter a patio in summer, yet allow welcome rays to penetrate on crisp winter days.

MICROCLIMATES

Light materials at noon
Light surfaces spread sun and heat.

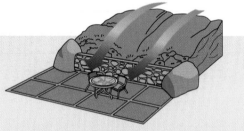

Downhill air movement
Cold air flows downhill like water, forming puddles in basins, which can be dammed by walls or solid fences. A sunken patio is often more chilly than its surroundings.

Dark surfaces at night
Masonry releases absorbed heat.

Deciduous plantings (summer)
Summer foliage shades the patio.

Deciduous plantings (winter) Skeletal branches let the sun warm the patio.

Possible Patio Sites

Often, people think of a patio as just a rectangle outside a back door. And if you have a small flat lot, that might be your best design option. But why not consider something a little bit more creative—a series of interrelated patios connected by steps, or a detached, protected patio in the corner of your lot? Perhaps you can accommodate a secluded patio in a neglected side yard. A number of options are discussed and shown in the illustrations over the next few pages.

Basic backyard patios: The standard backyard rectangle doesn't have to be boring. Edgings, raised beds, or gentle curves can customize and soften your design. Hanging plants and other amenities *(see pages 84-121)* can also help transform your space.

L- and U-shaped spaces: Houses in the shape of an L or a U offer prime sites for a patio. Surrounding house walls create a ready-made sense of enclosure. Privacy screens or overheads formalize the design. These patios are usually accessible from several rooms.

Wraparounds: A flat lot is a natural candidate for a wraparound patio, which allows access from any

A small front entryway becomes a welcoming brick patio. Flowering plants in a variety of unusual holders and pots add color and visual interest. Modest-sized furniture suits the scale of the design.

room along its course while enlarging the apparent size of your house. It may also help you use a wasted side yard.

Detached patios: Perfect for creating a quiet retreat, a detached patio works on both flat and sloping lots and is well suited to casual cottage garden landscapes. Provide access to such a patio by a direct walkway or a meandering garden path. Patio roofs, privacy screens, and a tiny fountain are all typical additions.

Multilevel patios: Large lots, or those with changes in level, can often accommodate striking multilevel patios, joined by steps or perhaps walkways. Such a layout is usually the best solution when you need multiple-use areas.

Rooftop and balcony patios: No open space in the yard? A garage rooftop adjacent to a second story living area might be an ideal site. Or consider a small balcony patio with built-in bench and container plants. Be sure your existing structure can take the extra weight of the wood or masonry (consult an architect or structural engineer). Slope the decking or paving slightly to allow efficient drainage.

Swimming pool surrounds: When the focus of patio living is a swimming pool, the setting can be formal and rectangular, or naturalistic,

A POTPOURRI OF PATIO SITES

The shape of your house and how your property is landscaped may dictate the best patio design for you.

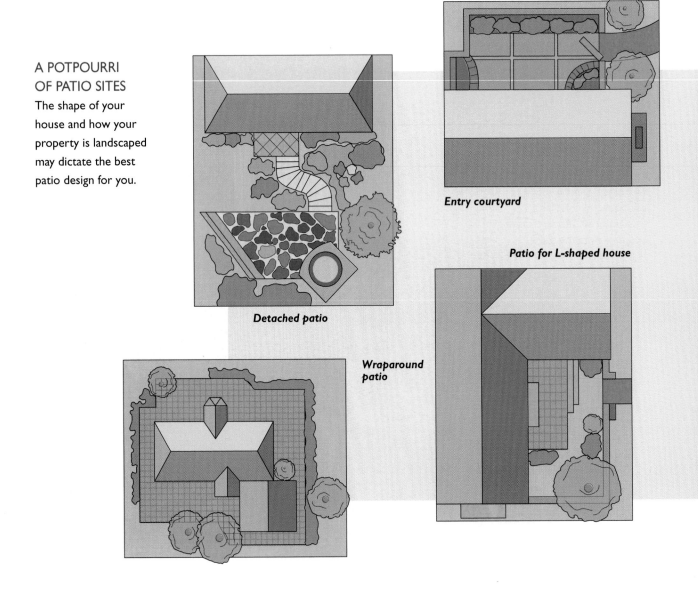

Detached patio

Entry courtyard

Patio for L-shaped house

Wraparound patio

with the pool blending into an informal landscape. Surround the pool with skidproof masonry and/or low-level wood decking. A patio roof, dining and cooking area, and spa are effective additions.

Entry patios: Paving, plantings, and perhaps a trickling fountain enclosed by a privacy wall can transform a boring entry path or thirsty front lawn into a private oasis. If local codes prohibit high walls, substitute hedges, arbors, or a trellis to let in air and light while blocking street lights and sounds.

Side-yard patios: A neglected side yard may be just the spot for a private, screened sitting area, which can brighten a small, dark bedroom or bath. If you're subject to local fence height restrictions, use overheads or arbors for privacy.

Sunrooms: A sunroom creates, in effect, an indoor-outdoor room. This is a great patio option for harsh climates. Some sunrooms can be opened up when the sun shines and battened down when the winter winds howl.

Interior courtyards: If you are designing a new home, consider the most private of patios—an interior courtyard, or atrium. If you're remodeling, perhaps your new living space could enclose an existing patio area.

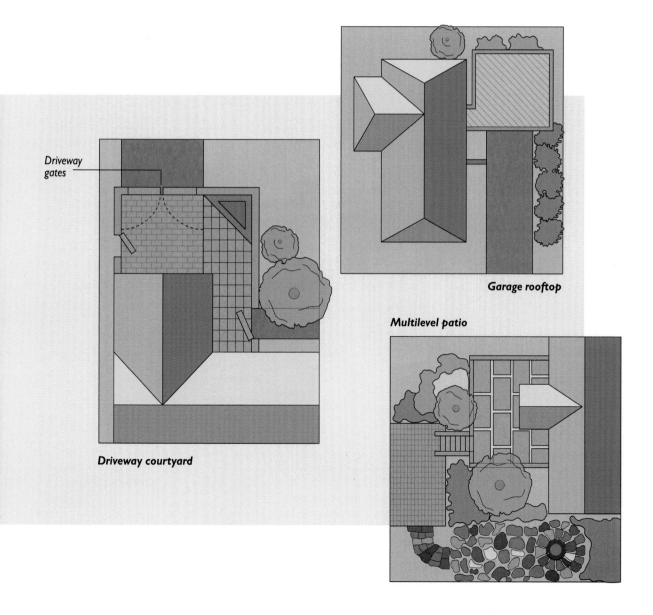

Driveway gates

Driveway courtyard

Garage rooftop

Multilevel patio

Patio-deck combinations: Homeowners in increasing numbers are discovering that patios and decks complement each other. The blend of masonry patios and low-level wood decking allows great flexibility in shape, texture, and finished height. Although masonry surfaces must rest on solid ground, decks can tame sloping, bumpy, or poorly draining lots.

Reclaimed driveways: You may have a masonry "patio" already in the form of a driveway. Sometimes driveways can do double duty as patios. Concrete turf blocks soften a driveway's appearance, yet allow for car traffic. Planted areas between flagstones or pavers achieve the same effect. Enclosed by a gate and accented with plantings, the area becomes an entry courtyard.

Existing slabs: If you have an old slab, you can either demolish it and start over, or put a new surface on top of it. Asphalt is best removed in most cases, but an existing concrete slab, unless it is heavily damaged, can serve admirably as a base for brick, pavers, tile, or stone; or you can top-dress the existing surface with colored or stamped concrete.

Depending on a property's micro-climate, the house can provide needed shelter from cold winds. This patio has the advantage of an accessible location—next to the driveway and just outside two doors. The brick paving is in keeping with the facade of the house.

A lush sun-dappled spot in a side yard can become a perfect place for morning tea. Plantings along the fence increase privacy and keep the enclosure colorful throughout the growing season.

Coming Up with a Plan

To turn your ideas into reality, take a long, careful look at your property. Even if you're remodeling a landscape you've lived with for years, this close examination may result in startling discoveries about what you thought was familiar.

DRAWING A BASE MAP

Use your observations about your site to create a base map, such as the one shown on the facing page. Be as precise as you possibly can; "guesstimates" or outright errors at this stage can result in disappointment later when, for example, you find that your new patio is in shade when you most want to use it.

Draw your base map (and later, your final plan) on 24- by 36-inch graph paper (1/4-inch scale). You'll need an art gum eraser, a straightedge, several pencils, and a pad of tracing paper. Optional are a drafting board, a T-square, one or more triangles, a compass, a circle template, and an architect's scale. For measurements in the landscape itself, choose either a 50- or a 100-foot tape measure; anything shorter is exasperating to use and can lead to inaccurate measurements. You can draw your base map directly on graph paper or on tracing paper placed over graph paper. Starting with the dimensions of your property and proceeding through all the information listed here, you'll gradually be covering a good deal of your paper with written and sketched details, so make each entry as neat and concise as possible.

You can save yourself hours of data gathering at this point by obtaining much of your information from your deed map, house plans, or a contour map of your lot. If you don't have these at hand, see if they're available at your city hall, county office, title company, bank, or mortgage company.

The specific information below should appear in one form or another on your base map.

Boundary lines and dimensions: Begin by outlining your property accurately and to scale, and mark the relevant dimensions on the base map.

The house: Show your house precisely and to scale within the property. Note all doors to the outside and the direction that each opens, the height above ground of all lower windows, and all overhangs.

Take time to evaluate the architectural style of your house; even if it fits no category neatly, you can probably establish its relative level of formality. What are its visual pluses and minuses? Later, you'll use this information to decide whether to camouflage or highlight particular aspects. At later planning stages, you'll want to keep attractive views open, maybe even accentuate them, and screen unattractive ones.

Exposure: Draw a north arrow, with the help of a compass; then note on your base map shaded and sunlit areas. Also note the microclimates—hot and cold spots and windy areas. Indicate the direction of the prevailing wind and any spots that are especially windy and may require protection of some sort.

Utilities and easements: Show the locations of hose bibs and the depths and locations of all underground lines, including the sewage line or septic system. If you're contemplating planting tall trees or constructing a patio overhead or gazebo, show the locations and heights of all overhead lines.

If your deed map shows any easements, note them accurately on your base map and check restrictions limiting their development.

Downspouts and drain systems: Mark the locations of all downspouts and any drainage tiles, drainpipes, or catch basins.

Gradient: Note high and low points with contour lines (here's where

COMPUTER PLANNING

In recent years there has been a boom in home-design computer software. These products are basically menu-driven, object-oriented drawing programs. With them you can enter your basic ideas and sort them out with the help of on-screen grids and rulers, as well as features that generate shapes and patterns and fill in colors. Home-design programs have the advantage of producing much clearer and more detailed plans than those drawn on graph paper with a pencil. However, since the programs can be somewhat difficult to learn, they will not necessarily save you time. As a rule, the bigger the project the more sense it makes to consider using one of these programs.

the official contour map is helpful). If drainage crosses boundaries, you may need to indicate the gradient of adjacent properties as well, to ensure that you're not channeling runoff onto your neighbor's property.

For small, nearly level sites, you can measure slope with a level and a straight board, as shown on page 134. More complex jobs may call for a builder's transit—and the know-how to use it.

Drainage: Surface drainage corresponds to gradient. Where does the water from paved surfaces drain? Note where drainage is impeded leaving soil soggy, and whether runoff from steep hillsides is rapid enough to cause significant erosion.

Existing plantings: If you plan to remodel an existing landscape, note any plantings that you want to retain or that would require a major effort to remove.

Views: Note all views, attractive and unattractive, from every side of your property—they can affect the enjoyment of your patio. Also take into account views into your yard from neighboring houses or streets. While screens and overheads may ensure some privacy, they may not impede the view from a neighbor's second-story windows. Note vantage points where relevant.

The environs: Step back a bit further and consider some larger factors before completing your base map. What are the visual characteristics of your neighborhood? Are there prevailing landscape and architectural styles?

Finally, note on your map the relation of the street and its traffic to your house.

A SAMPLE BASE MAP

A preliminary step in any landscaping project is to draw a base map—a scale drawing showing the important features and characteristics of the property.

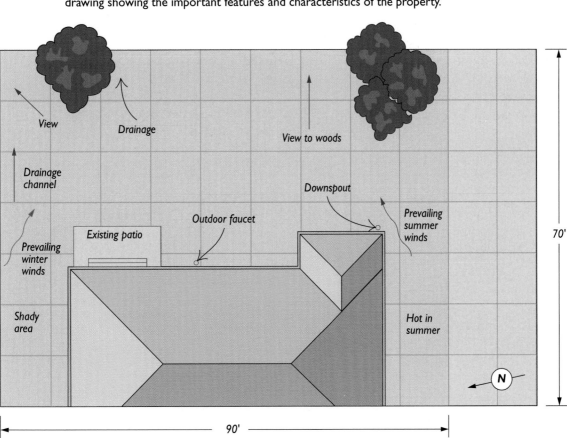

LAYING THE PROPER GROUNDWORK

Integral to designing a patio is observance of the "lay of the land," specifically grading and drainage.

Grading: Whenever you can fit any landscape element into the existing topography with little or no disturbance of the soil, you'll save effort, time, and expense. However, that isn't always possible. More often, the existing topography has inherent problems, or you'll need to alter it to suit your plans. Then you must grade the land: reshape it by removing soil, filling in with soil, or both. *(See page 126 for specific building techniques.)*

Aside from such practical considerations as ensuring good surface drainage, grading is often required for esthetic reasons. Perhaps an uneven spot destined to become a barbecue area needs smoothing out. Or maybe you've opted for an Oriental-style garden that calls for the creation of interesting contours. Frequently, flat, open landscapes cry out for vertical dimension: sculpting a berm near a patio will add that dimension, as well as create privacy and make your yard more attractive.

If your property lies on a slope so steep that, without skillful grading and terracing, it would remain unstable and useless, consider constructing one or a series of retaining walls. The safest way to build the wall is to place it at the bottom of a gentle slope, if space permits, and fill in behind it with soil. That way you won't disturb the stability of the soil. Otherwise, the hill can be held either with a single high wall or with a series of low retaining walls that form terraces. The drawing on the facing page shows various grading techniques.

Who should do the job? If the grading is simple and you have the time and inclination to do the work, you can save money and have the satisfaction of literally shaping the land you'll live with for years to come. But many special situations— for example, a high retaining wall— require that you obtain professional help. (Consult your local building department for the restrictions that apply in your area.)

If a steep or unstable slope requires terracing, contact a landscape architect or soils engineer, someone who can foresee all the

DRAINAGE OPTIONS

A uniform slope, as shown at right, directs water away from house; hilly yards and retaining walls may call for a central catch basin.

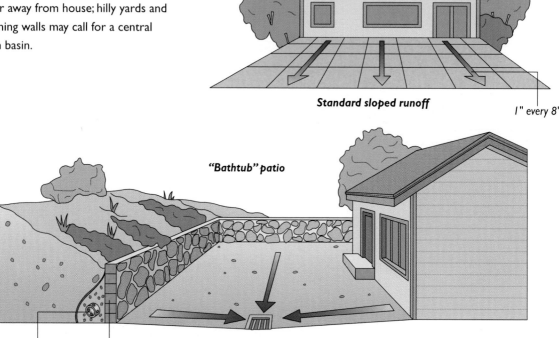

Standard sloped runoff

1" every 8'

"Bathtub" patio

Drainpipe — Retaining wall — Catch basin

implications and who is familiar with your local legal requirements. In short, you should rely on the expertise of professionals for major grading, including the grading of any unstable area.

Drainage: At the same time that you're studying the land's grade, you'll also be looking at its drainage. Wherever drainage is a problem, note the area and the solution, if you can determine it, on your base map and final sketches. For information on specific methods for improving drainage, see page 135.

If your landscape is nearly flat, it must have adequate surface drainage: a minimum slope of 1 inch per 8 feet of paved surface, or nearly 3 inches per 10 feet of unpaved ground. Steeper gradients are better for slow-draining, heavy soils.

Always route water away from your house, using one of the approaches shown on the facing page. Where the property slopes toward the house, you'll probably have to shore it up with a retaining wall, slope the surfaces inward as shown, and direct runoff to a central drain. Rapid runoff from roofs and paved surfaces sometimes requires a special solution, such as drain tiles or a catch basin.

Steep slopes absorb far less rainwater than flat areas and may drain fast enough to cause erosion. To retard erosion, such slopes need terracing and, sometimes, special structures. Appropriate ground covers and other plantings can also be used to slow runoff. Subsurface drainage, or percolation, is the downward penetration of soil by water; it's slow in clay soils, compacted surface soils, soils with mixed layers and interfaces, and soils overlying hardpan. Poor subsurface drainage is also a problem where the water table is close to the surface. Plastic drainpipes or dry wells offer solutions in many cases; a major problem calls for a sump pump.

On steep clay slopes most water runs off; nevertheless, retained water can cause mud slides. Get professional help to plan and install a drainage system for such hillsides.

GRADING OPTIONS

Grading for steps and retaining walls requires cutting and filling. Several solutions are shown here.

Retaining walls: three options

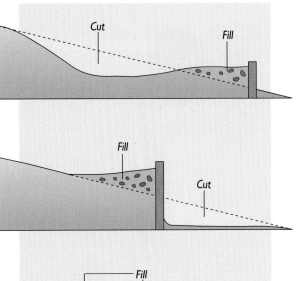

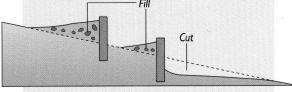

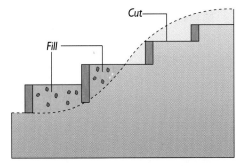

Step grading

EXPERIMENTING WITH YOUR IDEAS

With your base map completed, you can now try out your ideas. As you sketch, you'll begin to work out use areas and circulation patterns, and make decisions about what kinds of plants and structures you'll need and where to place them.

Here are some tips to make the design process more effective. Sketch as many designs as you can—at this stage, mistakes cost nothing. At some point during the process, your design will crystallize and you'll know it's final.

Think in three dimensions. This will help you balance the design elements and visualize the results.

Rely on familiar shapes. Landscape designs based on squares, rectangles, circles, and hexagons almost always generate results that are pleasing to the eye. Avoid arbitrarily curved patterns.

Try to see your design as a whole. Your patio is part of the garden and the house and will have an impact on both. If, for instance, you plan a patio off the living room shaded by an attached patio roof, will the roof make the living room too dark?

Experiment directly on the landscape by pacing off areas or using chairs or stakes to help visualize spaces and distances. Walk through planned traffic paths; bounce your ideas off others who know the site.

Defining use areas: Make a list of planned use areas and keep it in front of you as you draw.

For each design attempt, use a separate sheet of tracing paper placed over your base map, sketching "balloons"—rough circles or ovals—to represent the location and approximate size of each use area *(below)*.

As you draw, concentrate on logical placement and juxtaposition. Are you locating a children's play area in full view of your living area?

Plan generously—you can cut back later if the plan becomes too costly. Creating a strong design now will help you distinguish between the more and less important elements of your plan.

CREATING A BALLOON SKETCH

Place tracing paper over your base map; then draw circles for use areas and other features.

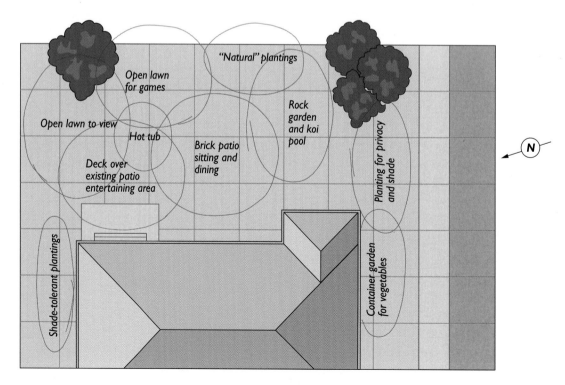

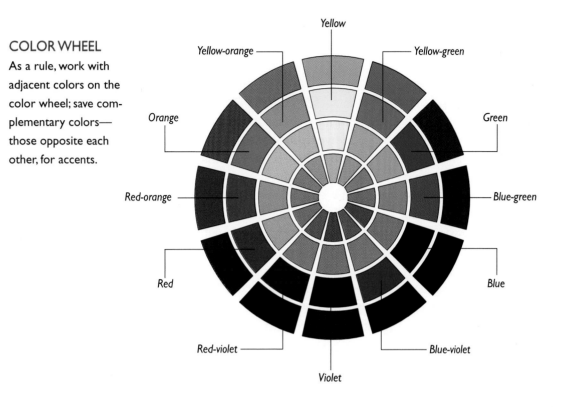

COLOR WHEEL

As a rule, work with adjacent colors on the color wheel; save complementary colors—those opposite each other, for accents.

Labels around the wheel: Yellow, Yellow-orange, Yellow-green, Orange, Green, Red-orange, Blue-green, Red, Blue, Red-violet, Blue-violet, Violet

---

Examining circulation patterns: Visualize foot-traffic connections between the various patio use areas, as well as to the house and yard. Will too much traffic be channeled through areas meant for relaxation? Can guests move easily from the entertainment area into the backyard? Consider whether the lawn mower or garden cart can be moved from the toolshed to the lawn without disturbing someone's repose.

When planning pathways, steps, and other routes, you'll need to figure in at least the established minimum clearances. Main pathways need to be at least 4 to 5 feet wide, service pathways, 2 to 3 feet.

Using color: The colors in an attractive landscape stand in a coordinated relationship to one another. Keep color in mind, then, as you choose materials. Brick, adobe, wood, and stone have distinctive, generally earthy colors. And don't forget that the materials you're using on your patio should blend with the colors of your house.

Even plants on or around your patio should combine harmonious colors, representing a continuous segment of the color wheel: red, red violet, and violet, for example (*see above*). The smaller the area, the narrower the color-wheel segment should be. Remember that not all foliage is simply "green"; the range of green shades is actually quite wide, providing lots of variety.

Choosing structural elements: Look closely at the successful patio designs shown at the beginning of the book. What elements do you need to include to create your own ideal outdoor environment? What materials will you use? (Before deciding, you may want to scan the information on building techniques on pages 126 to 179.)

As you begin to firm up your design, check to make sure you have covered all the elements on this checklist:

• Paving material or materials
• Edgings where appropriate
• Retaining walls for hills or slopes
• Walkways and footpath
• Steps or stairs
• Walls, fences, or screens for privacy and noise control
• Doors for access from the house.

Choosing amenities: Although some finishing touches, such as outdoor benches and planters, can be added later, now is the best time to think about the amenities you want and to sketch them on your design. Look through Chapter 4 for inspiration.

DESIGNING THE MODULAR WAY

Sometimes it's helpful to work with a single unit of space—such as a square or rectangle—repeated over and over again like squares on a checkerboard. Uniform design units help you be more exact in planning and give a sense of order to your design. You'll also find modules helpful when estimating materials—just figure the materials for one module and then count the units up to arrive at an overall total.

Modular planning is especially advantageous if you're laying patio paving for the first time. Concrete can be mixed and placed in rectangles or squares; bricks and other masonry units can be laid one rectangle at a time. Most professionals suggest a module that's no less than 3 feet by 3 feet.

To find out what size you should use, measure the length of the house wall that adjoins your proposed patio site. If it's 24 feet long, six 4-foot rectangles will fit your wall dimension exactly. If you plan to work with brick, tile, or adobe blocks, make your module an exact multiple of their dimensions (be sure to include space for open joints if they're to be set in mortar).

Suppose, for example, you decide to work with a 5-foot square. The illustration at right, shows how your patio can be divided. The low-level deck is 15 by 30 feet (3 by 6 modules); the adjacent masonry patio is 15 feet by 25 feet. Note that the length of privacy screens will also be a multiple of 5, walks will be 5 feet wide, planting beds, 5 feet across, and tree wells will be either 5 feet by 5 feet or 5 feet by 10 feet.

SLIDE-PROJECTOR PLANNING

In addition to the sketches you're making over your base map, consider using a slide projector to illustrate your ideas. You'll need slides of the area you want to remodel, a projector, tracing paper, a soft pencil, and a fine- or medium-point felt-tip pen. (Video images can take the place of slides.)

Tape tracing paper over the image and sketch in the proposed changes. (With features such as doors, windows, roof, and ground lines already in the slide, it should be easy for you to maintain correct scale and dimension.) Use as many sheets of paper as you need.

When you're satisfied with your design, use a dark felt-tip pen to draw in the permanent existing background. Don't worry about capturing every detail.

Once you've decided on all features of a patio design, you're ready to make a final plan. This rendering is the final result of the design process; use it for fine-tuning, for estimating materials, and when talking with landscaping professionals.

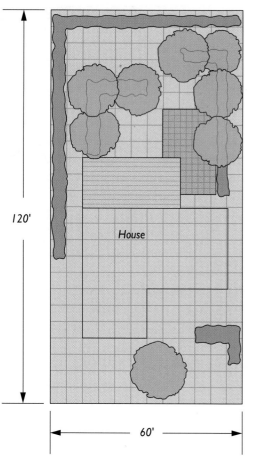

I square = 5'

MODULAR PLAN
Divide your sketch into uniform-size modules, then lay out patio, walkways, planters and other features in multiples of that unit.

120'

60'

House

DRAWING A FINAL PLAN

Most final plans include a plan view and elevation, such as the one shown below. The plan view is the classic bird's-eye view of the layout; the elevation, a straight-on view, shows how the yard looks to a person standing in one spot, looking in one direction. Complex structures, such as spas, retaining walls, or overheads, will probably call for additional details or cross sections (a slice through an object, rendered at an even larger scale).

Place a clean sheet of tracing paper directly over your base map. Label all of the features, as shown on the sample plan, trying to keep in mind what your plan will look like in three dimensions and in color. Make the plan as neat and concise as possible. If it is too cluttered to read easily, or if contractors will be relying on your plan, give your base map and final plan to a landscape architect or drafting professional for a final polishing.

Whatever your needs happen to be, remember that professionals are available to help you at every stage of the design and installation process.

A SAMPLE FINAL PLAN

The final plan is the end result of your design work. The main drawing, or plan view, is shown below left; a cross section (upper right) and detail (lower right) complete the picture.

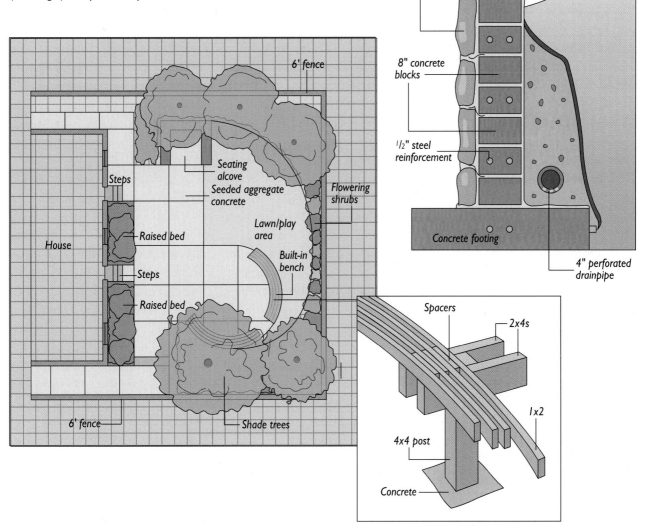

6' fence

Stone veneer

Mortar

8" concrete blocks

1/2" steel reinforcement

Seating alcove

Steps

Seeded aggregate concrete

Flowering shrubs

House

Raised bed

Lawn/play area

Steps

Built-in bench

Raised bed

Concrete footing

4" perforated drainpipe

6' fence

Shade trees

Spacers

2x4s

1x2

4x4 post

Concrete

Finding and Contracting a Professional

There are a number of professionals who can help with the design and construction of your patio.

PATIO PROFESSIONALS

Landscape architects: With one or more degrees in their field, landscape architects are trained (and in many states, licensed) to design both commercial and residential landscapes. They can help you set objectives, analyze the site, and produce detailed plans. Many are willing to give a simple consultation, either in their office or at your home, for a modest fee. They often can recommend contractors to do the work.

Landscape designers: Many landscape designers have a landscape architect's education and training, but not a state license. They can generally offer the same services as a landscape architect, and are often more experienced in residential projects.

Professional engineers: Engineers may need to be consulted if you're planning to build a structure on an unstable ground or a steep lot, or in a place where heavy wind or loads come into play.

Consulting engineers evaluate soil conditions and establish the design specifications for foundations and also design foundation piers and footings to suit the site.

Landscape contractors: Landscape contractors are trained to install landscapes: plantings, pavings, structures, and irrigation systems. Some also offer design services, which may be included in the total price of materials and installation.

Subcontractors: If you prefer to act as your own general contractor, you can hire and supervise skilled subcontractors for your project. Subcontractors can usually supply you with current product information, sell fixtures and supplies, and do work according to the specifications of technical drawings and the standards of local codes.

CHOOSING A PROFESSIONAL

The best way to choose a professional is to collect recommendations from friends and neighbors who have had work done and who will allow you to inspect the results. Keep in mind that some excellent professionals have no professional affiliation, while many belong to the American Association of Landscape Architects (AALA), or the American Institute of Architects (AIA).

It's important to check out all prospective builders. If you're working with a landscape architect, ask for the names of several contractors (or subcontractors, depending on your needs).

It's also a good idea to ask the companies you're considering for the names and phone numbers of a few of their customers. Call to find out if the jobs were done well.

Select three or four companies whose work you like and ask them to submit bids on your project. Have each bid on the same package you and your consultants have prepared.

CONTRACT CONSIDERATIONS

Without a signed contract, you'll have nothing but trouble. A contract is an agreement between two parties covering the performance of specified work for a certain amount of money.

A good contract protects both your interests and the builder's. It must be tightly written, describing everything to be done and by whom, as well as everything not to be done. Don't sign it until you read and understand all of it.

A well-written contract should contain the following information:

Plans and specifications: These must be in sufficient detail to allow no question as to the job at hand. A plan, drawn to scale, should be attached to the contract.

Performance: The contract should specify the work to be done and all materials to be used. The date that work will start and end should be stated (unless local weather conditions don't allow it), as well as any penalties to be added for late work.

In addition, the contract should lay down conditions for suspension, arbitration, and termination (under federal law, you have three business days after signing the contract in which to have a change of mind). The contract should also provide for any running plan changes at extra cost.

Costs and payment: Outlined in the contract should be the cost of the work, the payment schedule, and the question of ownership in case of bankruptcy.

Legal considerations: Legal provisions in the contract should include the validity period for the agreed upon price, responsibility for permits and zoning compliance, and

Local Regulations

Before you go far in planning your patio, consult your local building department for specific regulations. For certain projects you will need to file for a building permit and comply with all the appropriate code requirements. Also you need to be aware of local zoning ordinances, which can determine what and where you can build.

Code requirements vary from region to region, setting minimum safety standards for materials and construction techniques, helping to ensure that any structures you build will be safe for you and any future owners of your property.

These municipal regulations restrict the height of residential buildings, limit lot coverage, specify setbacks, and may stipulate architectural design standards you need to follow.

Be sure to get the required permits before you begin construction: Officials can fine you as well as require you to bring an improperly built structure up to standard, or even to dismantle it.

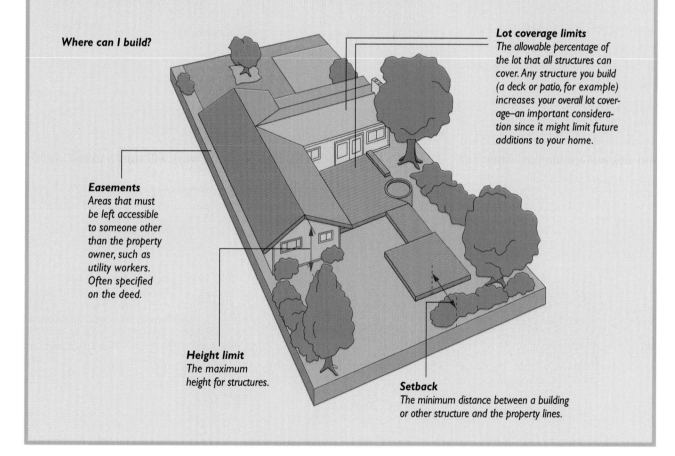

Where can I build?

Lot coverage limits
The allowable percentage of the lot that all structures can cover. Any structure you build (a deck or patio, for example) increases your overall lot coverage—an important consideration since it might limit future additions to your home.

Easements
Areas that must be left accessible to someone other than the property owner, such as utility workers. Often specified on the deed.

Height limit
The maximum height for structures.

Setback
The minimum distance between a building or other structure and the property lines.

provisions for lien releases every time you make a payment for labor or materials (these come from the contractor and any subcontractors and material suppliers involved in the project). The releases are necessary because even though you have paid the contractor, if he or she has not paid for the labor or for the supplies, you can be held liable for any outstanding amounts. You can also request that the builder post a bond assuring payment to all the subcontractors.

Liability for any damages and/or personal injury during the completion of the work and guarantee provisions for the contractor's work and any equipment installed should also be written into the contract.

Designs for a Small Lot

Suppose you have a flat, rectangular backyard that's nondescript and very small. That's the challenge we presented three landscape architects, each from a different locale, when we asked them to come up with a design for the yard. Our idea was not to illustrate a single "best" solution, but to show that for any situation there are a number of successful treatments. In addition to giving the landscape architects a thumbnail sketch of the yard shown below, we presented them with some information about the site and the owners. We described the owners as professionals in their early forties with two teenagers and no pets. The owners, we said, do not wish to make any structural changes to the house, but want to create a beautiful retreat with plants that are in keeping with their climate and water resources.

THE BASIC LOT

Not only is this lot flat and empty, but there are no special features or plants on the neighboring properties worth including visually. In fact, there are some undesirable elements: a second-story deck on the house next door, a shed abutting the back corner of the property, wood side fences that are in poor condition, and a neighbor's swing set and tetherball pole that are visible above an unattractive back wall.

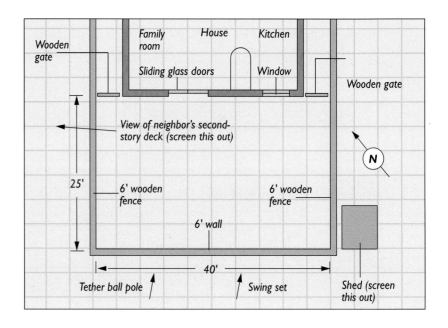

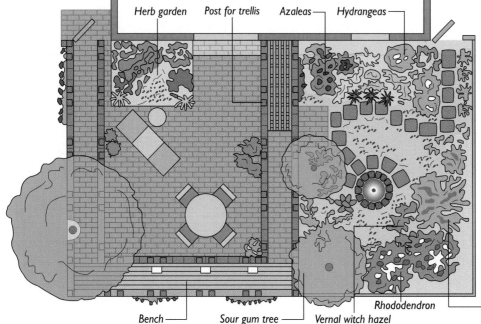

New England Appeal

An expansive light red brick patio off the family room looks right at home in this design; header courses of darker bricks echo the line of the lattice trellis enclosure. Azaleas and hydrangeas on one side of the door and a kitchen herb garden on the other add color. On the garden side, stepping-stones lead to a small stone pool and fountain. Two rhododendrons, a vernal witch hazel, and a kousa dogwood hide the shed; a sour gum anchors the opposite (southwest) corner. A bench with built-in uplights is tucked below the trellis along the back wall.

Landscape architect: Carol R. Johnson & Associates, Inc. Cambridge, Massachusetts.

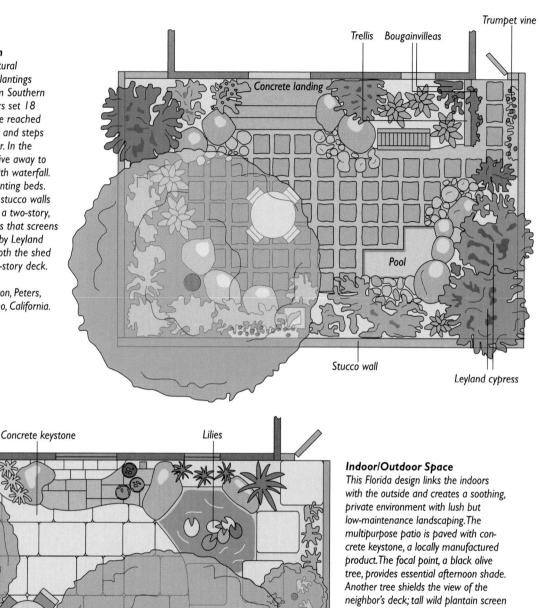

The California Solution

Local flagstone paving, natural boulders, and waterwise plantings distinguish this design from Southern California. Cut-stone pavers set 18 inches below floor level are reached by a cast concrete landing and steps softened by a large planter. In the south corner, the pavers give away to an angular garden pool with waterfall. Native boulders retain planting beds. Privacy is ensured by new stucco walls clad with trumpet vine; by a two-story, bougainvillea-covered trellis that screens out the eastern view; and by Leyland cypress trees that block both the shed and the neighbor's second-story deck.

Landscape architect: Eriksson, Peters, Thoms, San Juan Capistrano, California.

Trumpet vine

Trellis   Bougainvilleas

Concrete landing

Pool

Stucco wall

Leyland cypress

Concrete keystone   Lilies

Pool

Black olive

Indoor/Outdoor Space

This Florida design links the indoors with the outside and creates a soothing, private environment with lush but low-maintenance landscaping. The multipurpose patio is paved with concrete keystone, a locally manufactured product. The focal point, a black olive tree, provides essential afternoon shade. Another tree shields the view of the neighbor's deck; tall wild plantain screen out the shed. The gunite goldfish pond's bubbling waterfall soothes the eyes and ears. Water lilies float on the surface; keystone stepping-stones cross the pond. The new eastern wall is tiled with mirrors to expand the space. The other walls are covered with a variety of creeping fig, a close-growing vine.

Landscape architect: A. Gail Boorman and Associates, Naples, Florida.

Designs for a Large Lot

As with the small lot on the preceding pages, the designs shown here are landscape architects' suggestions for how to handle the sample lot below. This time, the lot is larger, with room for a few amenities and with a sloping grade that opens up a number of options.

The lot is empty except for a tree and a small concrete slab, neither of which the owners feel has to be preserved. A door from the living room leads out to the existing concrete slab patio. The bedrooms, several feet above grade in this split-level house, offer a view of the backyard.

Again, the hypothetical owners are professionals with two teenage children. They enjoy outdoor entertaining, but would also like space for private relaxation. They are willing to make a few structural changes to the landscape, such as installing a masonry patio, a wooden deck, or a spa or swimming pool. As well, the owners want to screen out the view of their neighbor's backyard on one side of the property.

THE BASIC LOT

Bare except for a tree and a small concrete slab, the lot slopes several feet to the house. Doors from both the family room and living room lead outside.

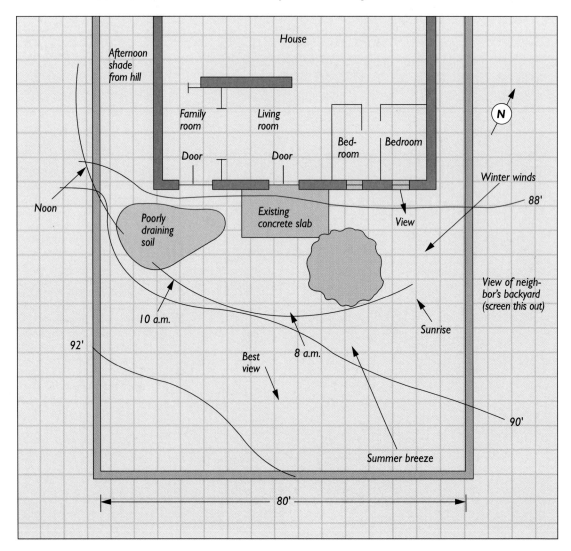

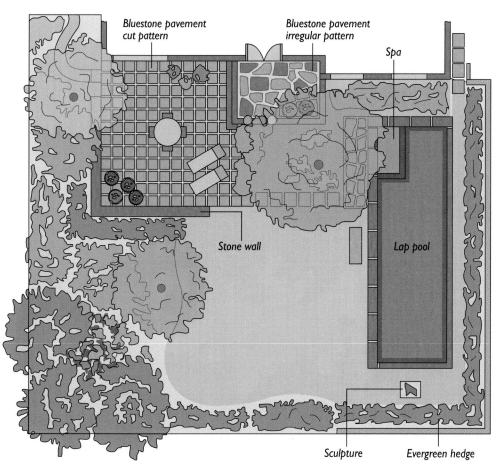

Bluestone pavement cut pattern

Bluestone pavement irregular pattern

Spa

Stone wall

Lap pool

Sculpture

Evergreen hedge

Neat and Orderly

Formal and precise, this plan has bluestone pavement in an irregular but highly crafted version off the living room and a 2-foot cut pattern for the main patio area. The large lawn and 12-by-40-foot lap pool with integral spa are major activity areas; here, the lot has been graded flat, and drainage provided. The lap pool reflects the sky; the sculpture at the end of the pool is an important focal point and can be viewed from the bedrooms. The hillside garden in the south corner, visible from the house and patio, provides texture and color, as does the perennial garden at the corner of the patio. A high evergreen hedge screens the adjacent property and establishes a visually protected environment. Stone walls set off the geometric patio area from the softer plantings.

Landscape architect: Stephenson & Good, Washington, D.C.

Many Spaces in One

This multispace, multilevel solution artfully combines a variety of materials and use areas. The principal patio surface is flagstone, accessed from the house by sliding glass doors. Beyond is an expanse of lawn—a possible future pool site—along with a private sitting alcove fitted with a built-in bench, and partially shaded by tall trees. Flagstones laid in sand provide the paving underfoot. Opposite, steps climb up to a wood deck equipped with a barbecue, a tiled serving counter, and built-in seating. The deck opens at the back to a boulder-edged natural pool and small waterfall. Behind is a second, more private deck, complete with a spa and an arbor with built-in towel racks and lights. Drought-tolerant plantings line fences and property lines; thirstier plants are near the house.

Landscape architect:
Ransohoff, Blanchfield, Jones,
Inc., Redwood City, California.

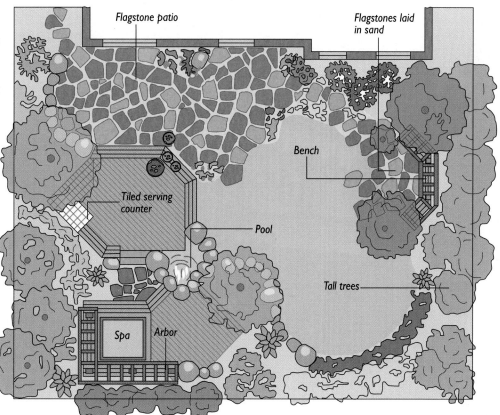

Flagstone patio

Flagstones laid in sand

Bench

Tiled serving counter

Pool

Tall trees

Spa

Arbor

Patio

ESSENTIALS

The average patio hosts a wide variety of outdoor activities. With the right amenities, it can be a breakfast nook, living area, reading room, and children's play area all in one. Before you get to the stage of choosing amenities, however, you'll want to select the more basic elements of the patio: its surface material, edging, and any stairs or walkways required to join the patio to the garden or to link different patio areas. Your choices for these essentials will largely determine the style and cost of your patio. In this chapter, we'll first discuss the basic elements that make up a patio, and then outline the patio surface options as well as the choices in steps and walkways. This information should help you create a patio that suits your sense of style, harmonizes with your house and garden, and respects your budget.

The stone surface adds a touch of casualness to this stately patio setting. Potted plants help tie the sitting area to the lawn and bordering garden.

Patio Elements

Patios are often defined by their surface material, and with good reason. Whether gentle, rustic adobe, warm, traditional brick, or sleek, stamped concrete, a patio's surface is its defining characteristic, giving it its charm and establishing its style.

The illustrations opposite show how the same patio area can take on a different look, depending on what surface material is used. In the remainder of this chapter, you'll find photos of the various patio surface options, along with descriptions of their properties, to help guide your choice for your own patio.

Although the surface is what strikes us most about a patio, there are other essential elements. Most patios have an edging, which serves both to visually define the borders and to physically contain the surface material.

Various effects are possible with edgings. For example, you can subtly define the borders of a brick patio by using bricks placed on end as the edging, or, to boldly emphasize the patio's outline, choose wood stained a contrasting color to the bricks. Some patio materials, such as stone, are structurally stable without edgings so you can create a patio that blends seamlessly into the surrounding lawn or garden. For more on edgings, turn to page 77.

A properly constructed foundation is also an essential element in a well-constructed patio. Depending on the surface material you choose, an appropriate foundation may be a sand bed, a concrete slab, or even stable, undisturbed soil. No matter what type of foundation is used, careful preparation is crucial for a long-lasting patio. The various options are discussed in the chapter on building techniques beginning on page 126.

In some cases, steps and walkways can be an essential part of a patio plan. A walkway is basically just a long, narrow patio, and may

---

SELECTING THE SURFACE

Here are some factors to keep in mind when you're choosing the patio's surface material.

• **Surface texture:** Smooth, shiny surfaces can be slippery when wet, and rougher ones too absorbent for use where spills are likely, such as near a barbecue. Smooth surfaces are best for dancing; games require surfaces with more traction. A soft surface is fine for foot traffic, but a hard-wearing surface is a must in areas furniture may be dragged across.

• **Appearance:** Consider your taste in color, texture, pattern, and reflective quality. Dull surfaces mean less glare on the sunny side of the house; shiny surfaces can catch the light on the shady side.

• **Maintenance:** Most surfaces can be simply hosed down or swept, but some may show dirt more than others and need attention more often. Large mortar joints may trap debris, but shed water easily. Sand joints are easy to maintain but may allow weeds to grow through.

• **Durability:** Consider wear from both climate and use. On stable soil, bricks set in sand make a permanent patio, but in areas with extreme freezing, you'll need to rework the bricks every so often, possibly even every spring.

• **Cost:** It's not just the cost of the materials that affects the cost of a patio. If you want a material not common in your area, for example, you'll have to include the cost of having it shipped from elsewhere. Labor costs may vary for the different installation methods. For some materials, you may be able to save labor costs altogether by doing all or some of the work yourself.

be all you need to unify other structural elements. An example of this would be connecting the existing deck near the house with a new water garden planned in a far corner of the yard.

Steps may be crucial elements, especially on a sloping lot. If you decide to level an area for a patio, you may need a couple of steps to lead up or down to it. Sometimes, the easiest way to tame a slope is to build a terraced walkway, basically a series of narrow patios connected by steps, that rise one level at a time up the slope. Other ideas for steps and walkways can be found beginning on page 81.

PATIO PAVING CHOICES

The style of your patio, whether formal or casual, depends a lot on the surface material. Choose a material in keeping with the style of your house and garden. Various patio surface options for the same space are shown below.

Brick
This traditional surface harmonizes with many garden styles.

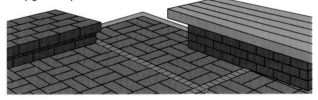

Adobe
Rounded, massive blocks tend to lend a casual feel, especially when softened with crevice plantings.

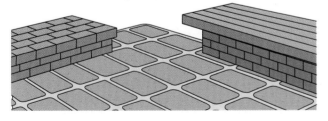

Cast concrete
Modern surface finishing techniques, such as coloring and stamping, can give concrete a variety of looks, from imitation stone to a sleek architectural finish.

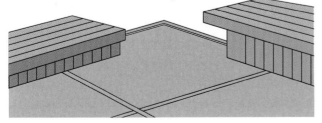

Loose materials
Very casual in feel, loose materials (smooth stones, gravel, wood chips) are usually less expensive, but also less permanent, than more solid materials, and they're harder to keep clean.

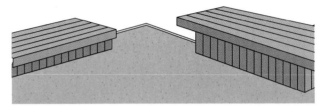

Interlocking pavers
These units are easy to install, and are available in contemporary patterns and colors.

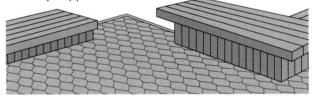

Tile
This is the right choice if you want a formal effect, with smooth, usually reflective surfaces.

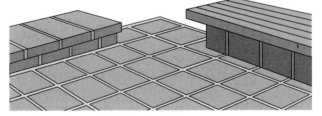

Stone
Stone can provide various effects, from rugged and rough-hewn to more formal, depending on color and shape of stones chosen.

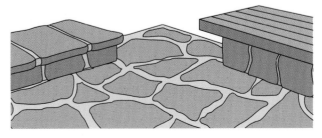

Brick

Brick is probably the most adaptable and frequently used patio surfacing material available. Set on sand or in mortar, brick provides a handsome surface that blends with nearly any architectural style and looks at ease in almost any setting.

Bricks are available in varied colors, sizes, and finishes and can be laid in a number of patterns, from the basic to the complex. You can combine patterns in striking combinations, to put an individual stamp on your patio. Some patterns and combinations are shown on pages 56 and 57.

Brick does have disadvantages, however. Cost per square foot runs higher than most alternative materials, and, if you lay bricks in sand, you may have to rework the patio from time to time if frost heave raises some of the bricks. Also, you may occasionally need to spend time pulling out weeds that have pushed through the joints. (This problem can be reduced by using landscaping fabric beneath the bricks.) A brick surface can be jarringly uneven if the bricks are poorly installed. Also, bricks in moist, heavily shaded garden areas can become slick with algae-like growth.

Brick types: Although the basic form and composition of bricks have remained unchanged for thousands of years, today's builder can choose from an almost bewildering variety of combinations of colors, textures, and shapes.

Bricks are made of various clay and shale mixtures. Originally, all bricks were molded by hand, but modern brick-making methods include extraction, in which the clay is forced through a die and then cut with wires into brick-size pieces. Bricks are first carefully dried and then fired in a kiln at very high temperatures so that they become permanent. The firing process, although much improved over the last century, still produces some bricks, called clinkers, that have irregularities caused by inappropriate firing. They may have surface irregularities and "flashed" patches from over-burning. Clinkers can be used for paving or as accents. They give a rough cobblestone effect.

Two basic kinds of bricks are usually used for garden paving: common brick, which has a rough texture, and face brick, which is slick. People like the familiar color and

BRICK PAVER CHOICES

Below are some of the many options in paving bricks. Common brick pavers have a rough surface that offers good traction. Used bricks may be difficult to find but manufactured new look-alikes are available. Bullnose bricks can be used for pool copings or stair treads.

Molded brick, made to look like cobblestone

Repressed chamfered brick

Flashed brick

Bullnose brick

Used brick

Common brick

New brick, made to look used

Plantings growing between the bricks soften the look of this brick-in-sand patio, making it seem like an organic part of the lush garden.

texture of common brick, and it has the undoubted advantage of being less expensive than face brick. Common bricks are more porous than face bricks and less uniform in size and color (they may vary as much as 1/4 inch in length).

The rough surface of common brick creates a nonglare surface with good traction. The surface is porous and readily absorbs water. As the water evaporates, it cools the air and makes the surface feel cool underfoot. Unfortunately, it will just as readily absorb spilled beverages, oil, grease, and paint, all of which may be difficult to remove. In addition, in freezing climates, this absorbed moisture can cause the bricks to be damaged.

Most brickyards carry two types of common brick, other than clinkers. Wire-cut brick is square cut and has a rough texture with little pit marks on its face; lay it to expose the edge if you want a smooth surface. Sandmold brick is slightly larger on one side because it must be turned out of a mold; it is smooth textured and easy to keep clean.

Face brick, which is manufactured to meet certain specifications, is used more frequently for facing walls and buildings than for residential paving. Face brick does make very attractive accents, edgings, header courses, stair nosings, and raised beds—use it anywhere, providing its smooth surface does not present a safety hazard.

Used brick, which may be common or face, has uneven surfaces and streaks of old mortar that can make an attractive informal pavement. Taken from old buildings and walls, these bricks are usually in short supply. Many manufacturers are now creating new bricks that look like used bricks by chipping them and splashing them with mortar and paint. Manufactured used bricks cost about the same as the genuine article and are easier to find; they're also more consistent in quality than most older bricks.

Low-density firebrick, blond colored and porous, provides interesting accents, but doesn't wear as well as general paving.

Precut bricks are a boon for the do-it-yourselfer venturing out into more complicated bricklaying patterns. Tacks, quoins, bats, sinkers, traps, and spikes are just some of the traditional names for these special shapes. Cutting bricks to these shapes is an exacting task requiring the expertise of a highly skilled mason. Expect to pay about the same price per precut brick as for a full-size brick.

Brick sizes: Most brick is made in modular sizes—that is, the length and width are simple divisions or multiples of each other. This simplifies planning, ordering, and fitting. The standard modular brick measures 8 inches long by 4 inches

Brick Patio Patterns

A brick patio can harmonize with almost any style, thanks in large part to the range of patterns in which the bricks can be laid.

A simple pattern, such as running bond, has a timeless, understated look. A more intricate pattern, however, can make the patio surface the focal point. Intricate patterns can also add interest to the view of the patio from above, such as from an upstairs window or deck.

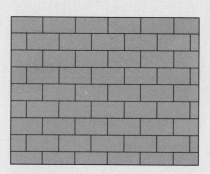

Running bond

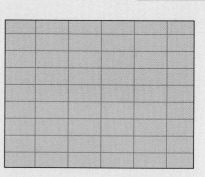

Jack on jack

Basket weave

Herringbone (45°)

wide by 2 2/3 inches high. Many other modular sizes are available at larger brickyards, in sizes ranging from 12 by 4 inches to 12 by 16 in various thicknesses. Note that all these dimensions are nominal—they include the width of a standard 1/2-inch mortar joint, so the actual dimensions of the brick are reduced accordingly.

It's common for bricks to vary somewhat from specified dimensions. Different colored bricks, even from the same manufacturer, may be slightly different in size. You'll want to keep these variations in mind if you're planning a complicated pattern with more than one color. Your building supplier can help you calculate the quantities of brick you'll need for your project.

Today, you can find many units larger or smaller than the standard dimensions that are excellent for paving. Such pavers are roughly half as thick as standard bricks. "True" or "mortarless" pavers are a standard 4 by 8 inches (plus or minus 1/8 inch) and are a big help when you're laying a complex brick pattern with closed (tightly butted) joints.

Brick grades: All outdoor bricks are graded by their ability to withstand weathering; if you live where it freezes and thaws, buy only those graded SX for use as pavers. Other grades recognized by the Brick Institute of America are MX, for applications where resistance to freezing is not important, and NX, for interior applications. Bricks are also classified according to the expected traffic load. Residential paving applications aren't usually subjected to heavy traffic, so bricks classified for low traffic loads should be fine.

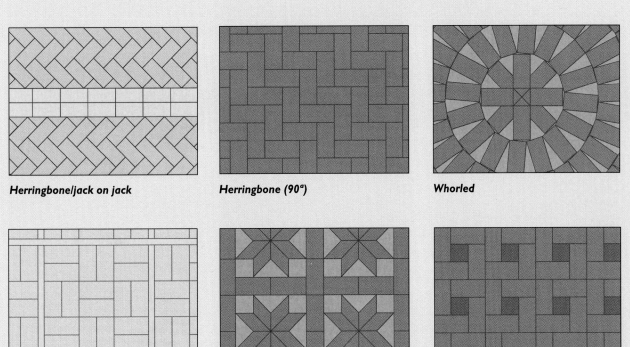

Herringbone/jack on jack

Herringbone (90°)

Whorled

Basket weave/grid system

Mediterranean

Pinwheel

Brick marries well with other building materials, as this combination of wooden steps and curved brick-surfaced landing and patio proves. Bullnose bricks, with their smoothly rounded front edge, give the landing a finished appearance.
Landscape designer: Walter S. Kerwin/Swanson's Nursery & Landscaping.

Bricks in three colors and whole and half sizes create an intricate plaid pattern in this courtyard. Doubled divider courses visually separate the pattern and add interest.
Landscape contractor: Richard Casavecchia/Architectural Garden Specialties.

Concrete Pavers

If your idea of a concrete paver is a 12-by-12-inch gray square, then you haven't seen the new generation of these versatile paving units. Paver manufacturers have transformed this patio material from a functional but aesthetically limited option into a viable choice for elegant outdoor paving.

Concrete pavers have been used in Europe for some time, for anything from public roadways to private patios, but their popularity was slower to develop on this side of the Atlantic. Fortunately, concrete pavers are now available in North America in a wide variety of colors, shapes, and sizes, and are being used increasingly in residential work.

Precast concrete pavers, like bricks, are an ideal do-it-yourself material. A weekend or two of work laying the pavers can result in a dramatic patio or garden walkway.

Pavers are available in two types, regular pavers, which have smooth edges, and interlocking pavers, which look somewhat like puzzle pieces and fit together in almost the same way.

Noninterlocking pavers are basically like bricks, although they're usually only about 1½ inches thick. Like bricks, they can be laid in sand, in dry mortar, or in wet mortar. Their main advantage over bricks is that they come in a wider variety of colors, shapes, and sizes. Aside from the basic rectangular shape, you'll find circles, squares, triangles, hexagons, and the specially shaped small pavers needed for complicated patterns.

Small pavers with interesting shapes can be used in combination with larger ones. A simple square can be part of a grid or even a gentle arc. Pavers can butt together to create broad, unbroken surfaces, or they can be spaced apart and surrounded with grass, ground cover, or gravel for interesting textural effect.

Shaped paver, for interesting patterns

Large-size paver, stamped and colored

Interlocking paver, specially cut for edge

Interlocking pavers, shaped to fit together

Rough-edged noninterlocking paver, for aged look

CONCRETE PAVER CHOICES

Shown at left are just a few of the many types of concrete pavers available today. Interlocking pavers come in a variety of shapes that can create a finished patio with an attractive pattern. Specially shaped pavers may be available for edges and corners, so that cutting is minimized.

Plain, noninterlocking pavers are essentially like bricks, but may be less expensive in some areas, and may be available in a wider range of colors and shapes.

Variations in the color of these interlocking pavers creates an elegant look; invisible edgings maintain the clean lines while securing the field units set in sand.
Landscape designer: Karen K. Steeb.

Of course, you can buy concrete pavers made to look like bricks, in classic red as well as imitation "used" or antique finish. In many areas, they may be significantly less expensive than the real thing.

Interlocking pavers, made of extremely dense concrete that is pressure-formed in machines, have contoured edges that fit into each other. When laid in sand (sand is also used to fill the butted joints), they form a surface more rigid than bricks. No paver can tip out of alignment without taking several of its neighbors with it; thus, the surface remains intact, even under very substantial loads.

Interlocking pavers are available in a number of colors, including tan, brown, red, and gray, and a variety of shapes that interlock in different ways. Specially cut pieces are usually available to fill in the pattern at edges and corners. These modern "cobblestone" patterns are very popular for casual gardens.

Turf blocks, a special paver variant, are designed to carry light traffic while retaining and protecting grass and other ground cover plants. These blocks allow for the possibility of grassy walkways and driveways, as well as side-yard access routes that stand up to wear.

Garden supply centers usually carry a good selection, of both regular and interlocking pavers, but availability may vary depending on location. Cost is determined by size and texture; for example, a 12-inch square of $1^{1}/_{2}$-inch-thick concrete seeded with pebbles can cost three times as much as a plain or colored paver of the same size.

When choosing colored concrete pavers, examine the options carefully; sometimes, the pigment is very shallow, and bare concrete may show through deep scratches and chips.

Some landscape professionals cast their own pavers in custom shapes, textures, and colors: adobe, stone, and tile replicas are just a few of the options. You can also make your own pavers, though they may not be as strong as standard units. Some homemade decorative options are shown on page 62.

The wide-open spaces in the overhead above complement the large-size concrete squares of the patio below.

Pavers arranged in ever-expanding circles seem to ripple out from the base of a small fountain; a smaller eddy marks the bottom of the steps. The specially shaped units needed for the center and first few rows are widely available.

Personalized Pavers

Concrete adopts the texture of the surface it's cast against, so by placing different objects in the bottom of a mold, you can create personalized paving blocks. A few ideas are shown below, but your imagination will surely create many more. Some materials, such as small stones, will stick to the concrete, while others, such as sand, will simply leave a surface texture.

Molds can be made from 1-by-2s, but if you're including material that will take from the thickness of the block, use wider lumber. The finished pavers should be at least $1^1/2$ inches thick. Finer patterns can be created if you cast with a $1{:}2^1/4$ cement-sand mix.

All molds, especially those involving moldings and small pieces of wood, should be liberally coated with form-release agent—available at concrete products centers—before casting begins. For a block with rounded edges that will easily release from the mold, press paste wax into all corners before casting.

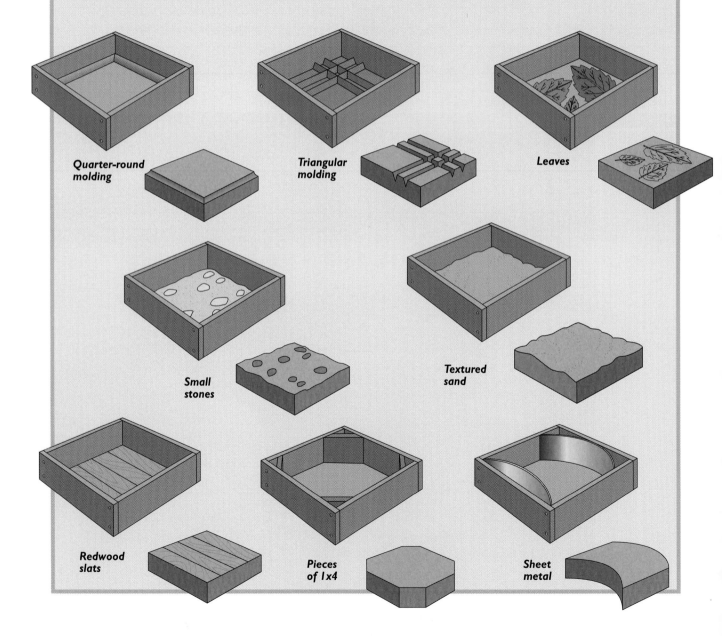

Quarter-round molding

Triangular molding

Leaves

Small stones

Textured sand

Redwood slats

Pieces of 1x4

Sheet metal

Stone

Stone pavers offer the warmth of a natural material, and most are very durable. Flat flagstones and cut stone tiles are ideal for formal paving. For a more informal look, you can use more irregularly shaped rocks and pebbles, setting them on soil or embedding them in concrete.

The availability of different types, shapes, sizes, and colors of stones depends on locale. Marble and granite are examples of igneous, or magna-formed, rocks; these are usually the toughest, longest-wearing options. Earth-toned sandstone, limestone, and other sedimentary stones are more porous; they usually have a chalky or gritty texture. Dense, smooth slate is a fine-grained metamorphic rock. Imitation stones come in many types and offer an inexpensive but attractive option to the real thing.

Generally, preparing stone for use as paving is a labor-intensive process—it takes a lot of time and effort to quarry, trim, haul, and store the stone. Even when found just lying on the ground, stone is a difficult material to handle and position. All of this makes stone an expensive building material, and price usually increases with distance from the quarry. But for many people, the beauty, elegance, and sense of permanence that stone offers make it well worth the extra expense.

Flagstone: Technically, flagstone is any flat stone that's either naturally thin or split from rock that cleaves easily. Flagstone works in almost any setting; its natural, unfinished look blends well with plants, and it's one of the few paving materials that can, if thick enough, be placed directly on stable soil. Its subdued colors—buff, yellow, brownish red, and gray—add warmth to a patio, and its irregularly shaped slabs contribute pleasing texture.

Flagstone does have some less favorable attributes. It is much more expensive than brick or con-

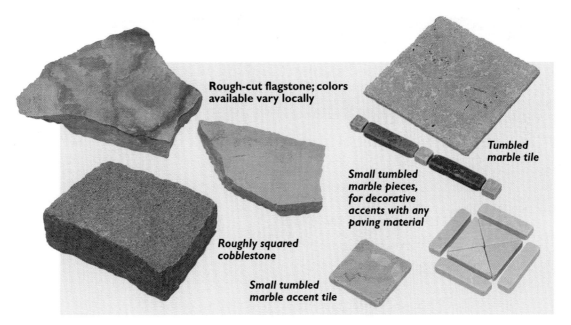

Rough-cut flagstone; colors available vary locally

Tumbled marble tile

Small tumbled marble pieces, for decorative accents with any paving material

Roughly squared cobblestone

Small tumbled marble accent tile

A SELECTION OF STONES

The stones shown above are only a few of the many options available for patio surfaces. Flagstone is a classic choice, both for formal and informal gardens. Its smooth, long-wearing surface feels cool underfoot, but it has enough texture to provide some traction, even when wet. Stones may be either irregular in shape or roughly squared into tiles. Roughly squared cobblestones make for a patio or walkway with an old-world feel and an interestingly textured surface. Tumbled marble, whether used for the whole patio or as an accent, offers long-lasting beauty with an old-world feeling.

crete and it's not a good surface for outdoor furniture, games, or wheeled playthings because of its irregularity. Also, some types of stone soil easily and are difficult to clean. Ask your supplier about the characteristics of the flagstone you're considering.

Flagstones generally range in thickness from 1/2 inch to 2 inches and must be laid out so there are no uneven spots and so the final pattern is pleasing. Without proper planning, including dry-laying the stones, it's easy to produce an unattractive patchwork effect.

Stone tiles: Many stone types are available precut to rectangular shapes. You can also find hand-cut squares and rectangles in random sizes. Slate, available in many colors, and granite are both popular, if expensive, choices.

Other stones: Fieldstones, river rocks, and pebbles offer alternatives to the high cost of flagstone. These waterworn or glacier-ground stones produce rustic, uneven pavings that make up in charm what they may lack in smoothness underfoot.

Flowering thyme softens the edges of these irregularly shaped flagstones. Different surface materials separate use areas in this large, multifunctional space.

River rocks and pebbles are widely available in countless shapes and sizes, are impervious to weather, and are virtually maintenance-free. Smaller stones and pebbles can be set or seeded in concrete; large stones can be laid directly on soil as raised stepping-stones. An entire surface can be paved solid with cobblestones set in concrete or tamped earth. Intricate patterns of pebble mosaic are interesting for small areas and narrow mosaic panels are very effective for breaking up an expanse of concrete or brick.

These options do have some negatives you should consider. Natural stones are very smooth and can be slippery, especially in wet weather. Because their shapes are irregular, they may be uncomfortable to walk on; this is especially true of rounded cobblestones.

Laying the surface, particularly when you're working with small pebbles and stones in mortar or concrete, is a very slow process. It's best to confine this surfacing to a limited area.

Smooth, waterworn stones meander through a multicolored sea of pebbles.

Pleasingly variable in color, these Idaho quartzite tiles make an elegant patio surface. Set in mortar on a reinforced concrete slab, these stone tiles will make a long-lasting patio surface.
Landscape architect: The Berger Partnership, P.S.

Adobe

The Southwest's version of the mud brick, adobe is one of the world's oldest building materials.

Although found almost exclusively in Arizona, New Mexico, and Southern California, adobe can be used effectively almost anywhere in the country. However, delivery charges outside the West can make it an expensive paving choice.

With its massive form and warm, earthy color, adobe creates a friendly, informal tone in a garden living area the way few other paving materials can. Because the blocks are large, adobe paving proceeds quickly, and your efforts yield immediate results. Adobe looks best when used in generous, open gardens, where the large size of the bricks will be in scale.

Set on a sand base and spaced with 1-inch-wide joints packed with sand or earth, adobe provides an excellent base for a living floor. Plant low-growing ground covers and moss in the joints to further soften the paving and blend it with the surrounding garden.

Historically, adobe structures were doomed to decay, eventual victims of the annual duel between summer heat and winter rain, although they could be protected somewhat by an occasional recoating using adobe plaster.

Today's adobe blocks, however, are stabilized with portland cement or asphalt emulsion, which does keep them from dissolving. Blocks stabilized with asphalt have a darker color than traditional adobe blocks; those stabilized with portland cement are closer in color to the original mud and straw bricks.

Adobe blocks commonly used in construction are made of essentially the same materials—soil, straw, water, and asphalt emulsion or portland cement—and have nearly the same textural quality. Some are formed in molds and air dried, while others are formed in a hydraulic compressor and can be used right away.

Adobe blocks used for building are generally 4 inches thick by 16 inches long, with widths varying from $3^1/_2$ to 12 inches. The most common block is 4 by $7^1/_2$ by 16 inches, about the same as four or five clay bricks put together. Blocks can range in weight from 12 to 45 pounds. In addition, a non-standard block has been designed specifically for paving use. Available in face sizes of 12 by 12 inches or 6 by 12 inches with a $2^1/_2$-inch depth, paving blocks may contain more stabilizer than is used for blocks in walls.

ADOBE

A traditional building material of the Southwest, adobe brings warmth and a casual feeling to patio paving. Two common adobe sizes are shown at right.

Square adobe block

Adobe paver

The rustic appeal of adobe, with its pleasingly rough edges and massive, earthy form comes to the fore in this gently curving garden path.

Tile

For both formal and informal garden situations, tile is a good choice. Tile looks as great indoors as out, so it's a good material to use on the surface of both an indoor room and the outside patio that's adjacent to it. This technique can create a feeling of spaciousness in the room, and, in the warm season when the connecting doors are open, the seemingly unbroken expanse of floor will encourage you and your guests out to enjoy the patio.

The warm, earthy browns and reds of terra-cotta tile blend well with natural outdoor colors, and the hand-fired pigments are permanent and won't fade.

Terra-cotta, which means "baked earth," is a good name for these tiles made of fired clay. Making tiles is much like making bricks or adobe blocks. Hand-molded tiles are individually shaped in molds, allowed to dry (often in the sun), then fired in a kiln. Machine-made tiles are extruded (pushed through a die), dried, and fired.

The color of the tile depends on the properties of the clay used and the firing process. The traditional orange-red color is a result of the oxidization of iron in the clay during the firing. Like bricks, tiles may be "flashed"—exposed to different temperatures in the kiln, which creates a mottled effect on the surface.

The strength and surface properties of tiles also depend on a combination of the clay and the firing process. Tiles fired at low temperatures tend to be softer and less dense, with a more porous surface, while tiles fired at higher temperatures are denser, with a slicker, glasslike surface. The more porous tiles absorb moisture more easily and therefore stain more readily; they may not be a good choice where spills are likely.

Glazed tiles have a thin glossy coating bonded to them in the kiln. The glaze may be colored and may have a variety of textures, from mat to pebbled. However, even rough-textured glazed tiles are slippery when wet, so they're not recommended for use as a primary surface material outdoors. They can be used for accents, however, or for edgings and raised planting beds. Glazed tiles with a special nonslip surface are available.

Terms you might hear used for the different types of tiles are "pavers," which is commonly used for hand-molded unglazed tiles, and "quarry tiles," which denotes glazed or unglazed machine-made tiles. Synthetic stone tiles mimic the look of granite and sandstone and generally have enough surface bite to be used on patios. Colors include black and various shades of gray and beige, with patterns of

TYPES OF TILES

From earthy to brightly colored and from rough to slick, tiles are great both for accent and as expanses of paving. The inventory below contains a selection of tiles commonly used in outdoor patios.

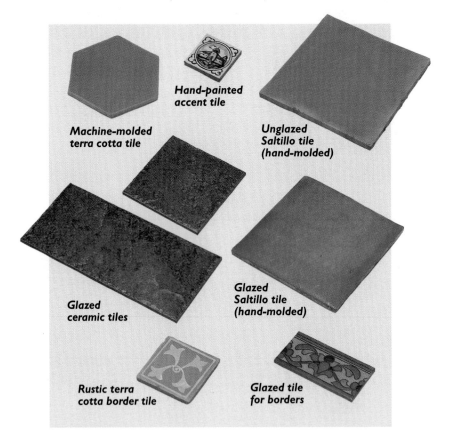

Machine-molded terra cotta tile

Hand-painted accent tile

Unglazed Saltillo tile (hand-molded)

Glazed ceramic tiles

Glazed Saltillo tile (hand-molded)

Rustic terra cotta border tile

Glazed tile for borders

Terra-cotta tiles, in classic earthy shades, create a warm, welcoming atmosphere in this entry courtyard. Darker tiles with rounded edges highlight borders and step edges. *Landscape architect: Ransohoff, Blanchfield, Jones, Inc.*

varying intensity. Concrete tiles, made to look like pavers or quarry tiles, are also available.

Tiles are generally a foot square or less, although larger sizes are available. Common shapes include squares, rectangles, and hexagons, but pointed pickets and other special shapes are also available.

Tile paving does have some drawbacks that should be considered before you choose it as your patio surface material:

• It's often quite costly compared with brick, sometimes two or three times as much per square foot.

• Because tiles are so hard, they're difficult to shape to fit the patio's design requirements.

• The surface of unglazed tiles must be protected by a sealer that should be reapplied periodically, a regular maintenance task that not all homeowners relish.

• The smooth, slick surface of some tiles, even unglazed ones, can give off harsh reflections and provide little traction when wet, a disadvantage around a swimming pool or spa. Such tiles would not be a good choice for any unprotected walkway or patio area, either, because they could be dangerously slick after a rain.

• Tiles, especially porous ones, are an ideal surface for mildew and moss growth, making them inappropriate for use outdoors in cool, wet climates.

Tiles should be mortared in place over a concrete slab. Setting tiles in sand is not recommended because sand is too flexible a base; the tiles will eventually crack, even under normal traffic conditions. Setting tile in concrete adds to the cost, but it's worth it: a well-installed and properly maintained tile patio is a hard-wearing, beautiful, and long-lasting addition to your landscape.

Loose Materials

For economy, good drainage, and a more casual look, consider including such loose materials as gravel, redrock, or wood chips in your patio plan. They will act as "filler" materials, both accenting and expanding the borders of your patio.

Gravel or wood chips can be combined with concrete pads, concrete pavers, or other stepping-stones. Gravel can be raked into patterns or set into decorative openings in other paving materials; or you can separate different gravel types with dividers. Loose materials also complement plants in transition zones between the patio and garden.

Unless compacted, loose materials are easily scattered and difficult to walk on. They also tend to be peppered with weeds growing through them. (You can greatly reduce this problem by laying the materials over a sheet of geotextile fabric.) They're not such a good choice under trees, because they tend to collect leaves, which are much more difficult to remove than from a smooth surface. All loose materials wear best when they cover a more permanent bed of pea gravel or decomposed granite, a somewhat grainy, clay-like substance that packs well. It's only available in some parts of the country.

By-products of lumber mills, wood chips and bark are springy and soft underfoot, generally inexpensive, and easy to apply. To work successfully as a patio surface, they should be confined with edgings.

Wood chips make a good cushion under children's play structures. Sometimes called gorilla hair, shredded bark is the most casual of these loose materials; it compacts well and is useful as a transition material between plantings.

Gravel is collected or mined from natural deposits. Crushed rock has been mechanically fractured and then graded to a uniform size. If the surface of the rock has been naturally worn smooth by water, it's called river rock. Gravels may be named for regions where they were quarried.

SACKS OF PLENTY

Loose materials are available by the sack or the truckload. Shown clockwise from the top are shredded bark, decomposed granite, redrock, river rocks, quartz pebbles, and redwood chips.

Consider color, sheen, texture, and size, and be sure to take home samples as you would paint chips. Gravel color, like paint color, will seem more intense when it is covering a large area.

Crushed rock compacts firmly for stable footing on paths and walkways, but its sharp edges may hurt bare feet. Smooth river rock feels better, but tends to roll underfoot. Small river rock, also called pea gravel, is easiest to rake.

Available under different names depending on location, redrock is a reddish, rocky clay that compacts when dampened and rolled. Along with decomposed granite, which is similar but longer lasting and more expensive, redrock can be put down alone or used as a foundation for another paving material. In time, the redrock surface will wear away, dissolving into dust.

Composed of carefully raked gravel and a few well-placed flat stones, this minimalist patio, like the Japanese dry gardens that influenced it, invites relaxation and meditation. Oversized wooden umbrellas continue the oriental theme.

Wood Paving

Few materials can match the natural, informal quality of wood. Wood may be used as paving in many ways: round disks can be embedded in random patterns in sand over gravel, square blocks can be laid like brick, or timbers can be combined with other paving materials or ground covers for a bold-looking, durable surface.

Rounds and blocks of wood will eventually have to be replaced, because the end grain is constantly in contact with ground moisture that seeps up through the sand or gravel bed. Choosing a naturally rot-resistant wood such as the heartwood of redwood or cedar will help. Pressure-treated landscape timbers, a less toxic alternative to used railroad ties, are another rot-resistant option.

Wood surfaces are sensitive to weather, too: they can crack and warp in sunny locations, or freeze and split in heavy frosts.

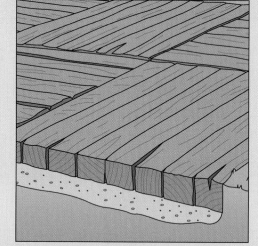

A patchwork patio
Pressure-treated landscaping timbers laid in a sand bed with sand brushed between the joints make a solid, natural-looking patio surface. A coat of stain with preservative will help reduce the visible effects of exposure to weather. Lay a sheet of landscaping fabric to contain the sand bed.

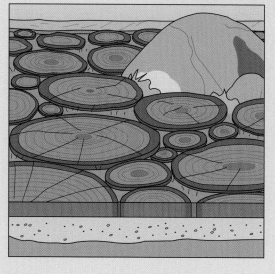

A woodsy walk
Sliced log rounds set on a bed of sand make for an informal garden pathway. Fill in the spaces with gravel or woodchips, or add low ground cover plantings as shown to enhance the natural feeling of the patio. For a longer-lasting path, choose rot-resistant woods such as the heartwood of redwood or cedar.

Cast Concrete

When it comes to patio paving, it would be difficult to find a more adaptable material than cast concrete. A mixture of sand, cement, gravel, and water, concrete is even more variable in appearance than brick. Using the proper forms, it can conform to almost any shape. It can be lightly smoothed or heavily brushed, surfaced with handsome pebbles, swirled, scored, tinted, painted, patterned, or cast into molds to resemble other paving materials. And if you get tired of the concrete surface later on, it provides an excellent foundation for brick, stone, or tile set in mortar.

Concrete does have some disadvantages. In some situations, it can be a harsh, hot, and glaring surface. If smoothly troweled, concrete can be slick when wet. For the do-it-yourselfer, concrete presents additional problems. Creating a top quality, good-looking cast concrete patio that will wear well and not crack or spall is more difficult than it might appear. The concrete must be mixed carefully to exact specifications; there's little room for error. Once

FANCY FINISHES

Giving a concrete patio a personalized look is all in the finish. Some options are shown below. The semi-smooth texture in (1) is achieved with a wooden float; the smooth, troweled surface in (2) is only appropriate for covered patios or walkways where it wouldn't get wet and become dangerously slippery; a broomed surface, as in (3) provides maximum traction. Three popular decorative finishes are rock salt (4), travertine (5), and seeded aggregate (6). Coloring concrete, either alone or in combination with other decorative finishes, can add a distinctive note.

1   2   3

4   5   6

Different surface textures create contrast in this large patio setting. The small raised platform, with its seeded aggregate surface and low, stone-faced wall, provides an intimate seating area within the larger smooth-surfaced patio. Wooden dividers serve as control joints, to reduce the chances of cracking, and add visual interest.

the ingredients are combined and water added, work must proceed quickly and accurately; mistakes will require extensive and, perhaps, costly removal and replacement. If the concrete isn't cured correctly or if drainage needs are ignored, the surface may buckle and crack.

Site preparation: Grading the soil and building the wood forms for the concrete can be quite a time-consuming procedure, but actually placing and finishing the concrete will go quickly.

The trick with concrete is to start small. Plan to divide your work into stages that you and one or two other people can handle. Cast large areas in smaller sections—that way, you can compensate for the large work crew and specialized equip-

ment that a contractor is likely to have on hand.

Casting an attractive slab that is itself the patio may be beyond your capabilities. But you might need a concrete slab as the foundation for another surface material, such as bricks or tiles. Where finishing the surface isn't important, casting a slab may be within your capabilities. Although the work is physically demanding and time consuming, it doesn't require as much technical skill as a finished patio.

If you're not sure you want to tackle the job yourself, you may be able to prepare the site and then let professionals take over. Be sure to discuss this possibility with any contractors you're considering for the job. Some may refuse to relinquish

control over any part of the construction process for fear that the work won't be carried out according to their standards. Keep in mind that once you agree to do some of the work, you'll be responsible for having your part done properly and on time.

Surface treatments: Concrete pavings are typically given some type of surface treatment, both for appearance and for traction.

Early modern architects often took a "warts and all" approach to concrete texture, reveling in the raw look left by rough surface finishing and construction forms. But the trend these days, at least for residential paving, is more toward careful, often subtle, finishing techniques that modify the look of the concrete so it blends more readily with its surroundings and with other building materials.

You can wash or sandblast a concrete paving to expose the aggregate, or embed colorful pebbles and stones in it. The second technique, generally known as the seeded-aggregate finish, is probably the most popular contemporary paving surface. Larger river rocks and field-stones can also dress up a dull slab.

Other ways to modify the standard steel-troweled concrete surface include color-dusting, staining, masking, sandblasting, acid-washing, and salt-finishing. Concrete can also be stamped and tinted to resemble stone, tile, or brick. The patterns simulate either butted joints or open ones, which can then be grouted to look like unit masonry. Coloring is a task that an experienced do-it-yourselfer likely could accomplish, but stamping is usually best left to professionals.

The domain of concrete finishing is a rapidly changing one, with new specialty finishes being developed every year. Contractors are the best sources of information on the options available in your area; contact a few to discuss the options they can provide.

Concrete with other materials: Uninterrupted expanses of concrete can have a cold, forbidding appearance, unsuited for the welcoming, warm atmosphere most homeowners desire in their patio landscape. To create visual interest, concrete can be blended with another paving material. Sometimes such designs also serve structural purposes. Control joints are a good example. They help prevent cracking in addition to serving as a visual design element that breaks up a large expanse of concrete.

Blending concrete and brick is a popular design option; tile and flagstone are other materials that complement concrete. Wood, steel,

Concrete marries well with other patio materials. Here, a brick patio close to the house shares the stage with a seeded aggregate concrete surface around the pool, where good traction is needed.

or copper dividers can act as control joints, as well as allow the do-it-yourselfer to divide the job into smaller, more manageable sections. **Creating a softer look:** Fortunately, there are several techniques that allow concrete to be used in a more casual outdoor environment. The surface treatments discussed earlier are a good start: coloring, texturing, and/or stamping all make concrete look more natural.

Another technique used to soften the look of concrete is to lay irregularly shaped chunks of broken concrete in a staggered pattern, with spaces between for planting ground cover. The broken edges and relatively consistent thickness of the concrete give the appearance of sedimentary stone.

You can also leave some open areas in a fresh slab, filling them later with soil and plants. Drip tubing can be routed to these pockets, to water plants thoroughly without soaking the surrounding paving. Another way to create a more casual look with concrete is to dig holes or shape curved forms to your own design specifications and then fill them with concrete. The resulting pads—with the spaces in between them filled with low-growing plants—can be smoothed, textured, and finished to resemble natural stone, or they can be seeded with aggregate or given some other special surface finish. Smaller free-form concrete pads make an attractive walkway; larger ones can make a casual patio.

Versatile cast concrete is a building material with a thousand faces. Here, it has been colored and tooled to look like stone. Referred to as architectural concrete paving, this technique combines the beauty of natural materials with the durability and relatively low cost of concrete. A licensed contractor in your area can help you select from a range of patterns and colors, or design a new one to suit your tastes.

Edgings

Although edgings may not be the most obvious part of a patio, they are nonetheless an important element. Edgings serve three main purposes: they contain the patio material—absolutely essential for units laid in sand; they serve as a transition between the paving and surrounding landscaping; and they are a decorative element in their own right.

Most garden edgings are made of wood, but brick or other masonry units, concrete, and stone are also used. You'll find instructions for building edgings beginning on page 136.

Edgings can also be used to visually link disparate elements in the landscape. Using brick to edge a lawn, an exposed-aggregate patio, and a gravel path, for example, will unify the overall design. Edgings can also connect different areas of a garden: a brick-edged patio, for example, may taper off to a brick path that leads to another patio area, again edged with brick.

Wood edgings: The most common type of wood edging is made of dimension lumber, such as 2-by-4s or 2-by-6s. Wood that's resistant to rot, such as pressure-treated lumber or the heartwood of cedar or redwood, is the best choice for edgings that will last as long as patio surface material. To make curved edgings, use flexible benderboard. Very tight curves can be formed

An edging of pressure-treated 4-by lumber holds this intricate pattern of concrete pavers in place.
Landscape architect: Lankford Associates.

with pieces of sheet metal or plastic; see page 141 for more information on curved edgings.

Heavy timbers make strong, showy edgings and interior dividers, especially when drilled and held in place with steel pipe, as illustrated below.

In addition to rustic timbers, you can use wood posts or logs, in diameters ranging from 2 to 6 inches, to form a series of miniature pilings. Set them vertically, butted tightly together, with their ends set underground in a concrete footing. Pack soil around the pilings. A horizontal 2-by-4 or 2-by-6 cap across the tops will prolong the life of the edging by keeping water out of the end grain of the posts.

Brick edgings: The easiest masonry edgings to build are brick-in-soil edgings. Bricks are set in a narrow trench around the edges of the patio area. As much of the brick as possible should extend underground below the level of the patio. Setting the bricks vertically is best, or angle them slightly for a toothed effect. Unfortunately, only very firm soil will hold the bricks in place without mortar, so brick-in-soil edgings are not possible everywhere.

Another option for brick edgings is the invisible edging, actually a small, underground concrete footing that secures paving units without any visible support. Paving units set into the surface of the freshly cast concrete conceal the

footing. The completed patio appears to have no edging at all.

When using bricks set in sand as the patio surface material, you can create an invisible edging by simply setting the edge bricks in wet mortar. This allows you to continue the pattern for the patio at a small fraction of the work and expense.

Casting footings for invisible edgings is relatively easy. The forms are small—just wide enough to take one brick—and the amount of concrete you'll need is fairly easy to mix and place. For more on building invisible edgings, turn to page 138.

Stone edgings: A rustic or woodsy landscape may provide a good setting for edgings made of cut flagstone or a more informal edging of

EDGING OPTIONS

Some patio surface materials, such as bricks or pavers laid in sand or loose surface materials, require an edging. But even when they're not structurally necessary, edgings add an attractive touch to a patio, defining its edges and perhaps visually unifying it with other landscaping features.

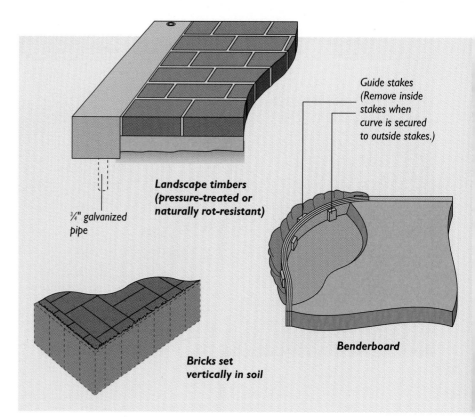

¾" galvanized pipe

Landscape timbers (pressure-treated or naturally rot-resistant)

Bricks set vertically in soil

Guide stakes (Remove inside stakes when curve is secured to outside stakes.)

Benderboard

rocks and boulders. If your patio design includes a garden pond, a stone edging around both the patio area and the edge of the pond can integrate the two areas, even if the patio itself is surfaced with another material.

Before laying flagstone or other small stones, arrange them in a pleasing pattern, cutting them if necessary. Then lay the stones in a 1-inch-thick bed of mortar.

Usually, large uncut rocks and boulders look best in edgings if they're at least partially buried; dig a hole to the appropriate depth for each stone. Otherwise, you can lay the stones directly on the soil, filling the spaces between with smaller rocks. Pack the area with soil and add plantings for a more natural look. Irregularly shaped stones blend well with loose materials. More formal paving units will probably need to be cut to fit around the boulders.

Plastic edgings: Manufactured plastic edgings are an easy-to-install option for do-it-yourselfers. The strips secure bricks or concrete pavers below the level of the finished paving. Once the paving is completed, the strips can be concealed with soil or sod, creating a patio that has no visible edging. Flexible sections are available for tight curves, but rigid strips can be made to handle gentle curves if you kerf, or cut, their edges. Secure plastic edgings with 10- to 12-inch spikes, or follow manufacturer's installation instructions.

Concrete edgings: Built similarly to invisible edgings, concrete edgings create a patio area with well-defined limits. Concrete edgings might be a good choice if concrete is used elsewhere in your garden, such as on a path leading up to the patio, or as mowing strips around planting beds.

A concrete edging serves to retain the paving units, but it also functions as a mowing strip, for a patio that's adjacent to a lawn. Running the lawn mower's wheels along the concrete edging will help you cut the grass right up to the edge of the patio, reducing the need for an edge-trimming tool.

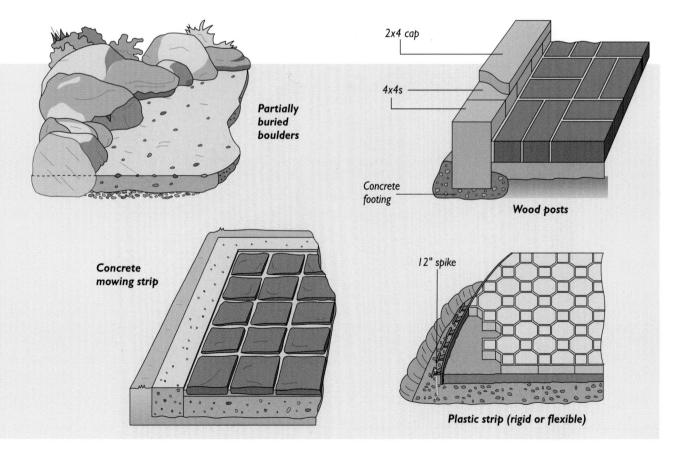

Partially buried boulders

2x4 cap

4x4s

Concrete footing

Wood posts

Concrete mowing strip

12" spike

Plastic strip (rigid or flexible)

Steps and Walkways

Garden steps and walkways may be an addition to your patio plan or they may be an integral part of it. If the patio occupies a raised area in your yard, a flight of steps leading down to the garden or lawn below would not be a luxury. And if your landscaping plan includes a variety of activity areas—perhaps a wooden deck near the house, a swimming pool or spa in the middle of the yard, and a freestanding patio in a quiet corner, a pathway connecting them may be all you need to unify the disparate elements into an attractive, coherent design.

Steps: Garden steps can be gracious accents that set the mood for an entire landscaping scheme.

Most inviting are wide, deep steps that lead the eye to a garden focal point; such steps can also serve as a retaining wall, a base for a planter, or additional seating space. To soften the edges of a series of steps, as well as help mark them for residents and guests, place plants in containers or in open beds along their borders.

Lighting around steps is an important safety feature, and there is an abundance of attractive outdoor lighting possibilities. You can make a bold statement, lighting up the edge of each tread, or go for a more subtle look by hiding low-

Redwood bark is a natural choice for a meandering pathway through the woods. For drainage and stability, lay bark or chips over a compacted base. *Landscape architect: Harvard & Associates.*

OUTDOOR STEP OPTIONS

Garden steps and walkways can connect activity areas together, tame the steepest of sloping yards, and visually unite disparate outdoor elements. A variety of attractive options are shown below.

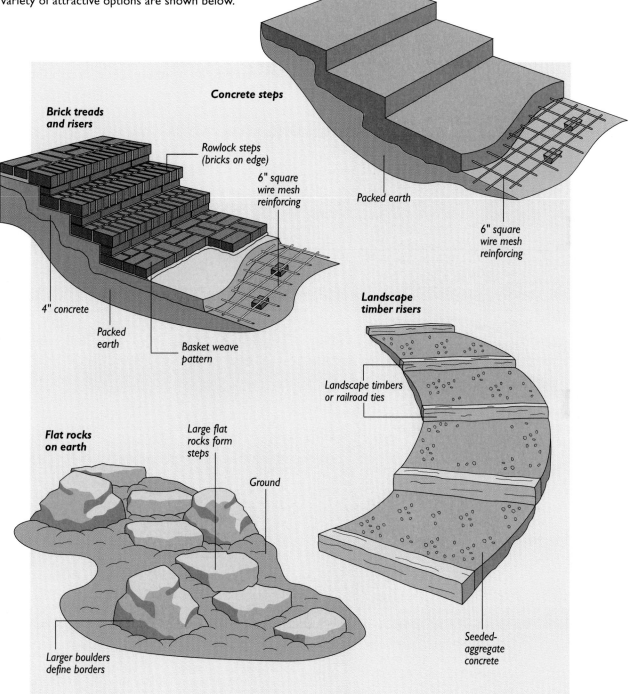

Concrete steps

Brick treads and risers

Rowlock steps (bricks on edge)

6" square wire mesh reinforcing

Packed earth

6" square wire mesh reinforcing

4" concrete

Packed earth

Basket weave pattern

Landscape timber risers

Landscape timbers or railroad ties

Flat rocks on earth

Large flat rocks form steps

Ground

Larger boulders define borders

Seeded-aggregate concrete

voltage lamps in planting beds along the sides.

Constructing steps of the same material used in the patio or garden walls helps unite an overall landscaping plan. Using contrasting materials draws attention to the steps and those areas of the garden they serve. Combining materials can effect a smooth transition between unlike surfaces. For example, you can link a brick patio to a concrete walk by installing steps with concrete treads and brick risers.

Regardless of the material you use, put safety first: choose a material for the treads that offers safe footing in wet weather, and be sure to provide adequate lighting.

Walkways: A walkway is essentially a long, narrow patio; the options in surface materials are the same, and the details of construction are identical. A walkway is often easier to build, because its narrower width makes striking off the foun-

Softened with mounds of flowering plants, long, concrete steps lead gently down from the patio. *Landscape architect: Robert W. Chittock & Associates.*

Lush plantings soften the edges of this basket weave patterned brick pathway. A small stone patio provides space for a seat along the way.

dation bed of sand or concrete much more manageable. It is also more feasible to build a walk in easy-to-work sections.

The shortest distance between two points is a straight line, but garden walks work best when this idea is ignored. But if utility is the main concern, a straight path may be best.

Whatever its direction, a walk is most interesting when it provides a series of experiences along the way. For example, it can alternately reveal and conceal special plantings, an interesting view, or garden sculpture. On a small lot, visual space is expanded when you conceal the pathway's end or use "forced perspective," gradually diminishing the width of the path to make it appear longer.

Keep appropriateness in mind when selecting materials. Major access walks should be made of brick, concrete, unglazed tile, or stone slabs for easy traffic flow and an even, nonskid surface.

Used brick steps and accents tie together the various elements of this comprehensive patio plan.

Making the
MOST OF
YOUR PATIO

*With the main structural elements of your patio in place,
you can turn your thoughts to the finishing touches and
amenities that will truly make the space your own. For shade
and shelter, it's hard to beat an overhead. In addition to
extending the number of hours you can spend on the patio,
it adds an attractive design element. A well-placed fence can
contribute to a feeling of privacy or even divide your patio into
use areas. Furniture is also crucial for comfortable patio living,
and should be selected with care. Other amenities include such
utilitarian features as a barbecue, efficient outdoor lighting, and
a heating or cooling system. Also consider decorative elements
like fountains, birdbaths, or flowering plants. Take your time
adding these finishing touches to your patio, so you're sure to
create the right space for you and your family. And who knows?
With the right combination of amenities, your outdoor room
could soon become the most popular room of the house.*

A few carefully chosen additions transform this small backyard patio
into an elegant garden retreat. The distinctive overhead echoes the
lines of a gazebo roof and frames wooden privacy screening. Lush
hanging plants add to the sense of enclosure, while sleek wrought
iron furniture makes good use of space.

Patio Overheads

An overhead can make a patio more inviting by providing much-needed shade; at the same time, overheads function as "space frames" that can define all or part of your patio.

The key is to design a structure that integrates well with the style of your house and suits the site.

Whether you want to design and build the structure yourself or hire a professional, this section will help you understand the entire process, from conception to completion.

In the pages that follow, you'll learn what factors you need to consider—site and weather, for example—before installing an overhead. If you're inclined to build one yourself, you'll also get a good grounding in how a freestanding overhead is built and how it should be planned to suit the style of your house. The section concludes with a gallery of overhead cover options.

This expansive, attached overhead throws welcome shade both inside the house and out, but is high enough above the patio not to seem imposing.
Landscape architect: John J. Greenwood and Associates, Inc.

A good overhead design should take its cue from your home's architectural style. If your house is Victorian, for example, lattice would be an appropriate material.

Though it's not essential that an overhead near your house be built from the same materials as your house, the new structure should blend with it, rather than creating a jarring contrast. Colors should be complementary as well.

For a house-attached overhead, consider the sight lines. Will the overhead block a pleasing view from the adjacent room, or make the room too dark?

Choosing a site: For many overhead projects the site is predetermined. However, if your site is more flexible, or you're developing a more comprehensive landscaping plan, consider different locations, evaluating each on its accessibility from the house, any established traffic patterns from house to yard, views you want to preserve from inside the house and out, and overall convenience.

At the same time, you'll want to maximize the assets of your property. Study its contours, views, the location of trees, and other relevant elements and factor them into the final plan.

Sun and weather: Shade is cast at various angles, depending on the time of year and where you live *(see map and chart on page 26)*. If you live in an area that experiences heavy snowfall, don't forget to factor in its effects. If you're planning to have a solid roof over your patio, for instance, you will need professional advice to make sure the roof will be strong enough to bear snow and ice. The charts below contain the maximum rafter and beam spans for patio overheads.

MAXIMUM RECOMMENDED RAFTER SPANS

The following spans are based on a load of 5 p.s.f. and No. 2 and Better lumber

Rafter size	Maximum Rafter Spacing		
	12"	16"	24"
2x4	10'	9'	8'
2x6	16'	14'	12'
2x8	20'	18'	16'

MAXIMUM RECOMMENDED BEAM SPANS

The following spans are based on a load of 5 p.s.f. and No. 2 and Better lumber

Beam size	Maximum Beam Spacing (or between beam and ledger)	
	12'	16'
2x10	10'	8'
2x12	14'	12'
3x6	8'	6'
3x8	10'	8'
3x10	12'	10'
3x12	16'	14'
4x4	6'	4'
4x6	8'	6'
4x8	12'	10'
4x10	14'	12'
4x12	18'	16'

A patio overhead, together with lattice panels fastened to three sides, creates a sheltered and intimate spot in a larger landscape design. Flowering plants in window boxes and hanging pots add accent colors.

BUILDING A BASIC OVERHEAD

The steps shown below are intended to give you a general idea of the building sequence for a freestanding overhead.

The main components of an overhead are posts, beams, rafters, and surfacing. If an overhead is attached to a house, a ledger replaces one beam. Roofing can take various forms *(see page 91)*.

Fasteners and connectors, such as post caps, strengthen the structure and make building easier. Post anchors hold post bases in place.

They can be set in a concrete slab just after the concrete has been placed. Post anchors can also be fastened to an existing concrete slab with expansion bolts, or to piers set outside the perimeter of the patio *(see opposite page)*.

Assembling an overhead frame

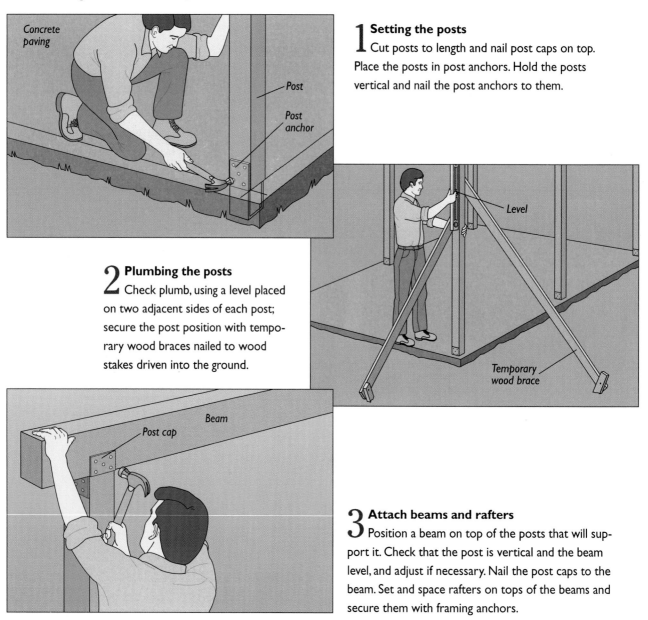

Concrete paving

Post

Post anchor

1 Setting the posts
Cut posts to length and nail post caps on top. Place the posts in post anchors. Hold the posts vertical and nail the post anchors to them.

Level

Temporary wood brace

2 Plumbing the posts
Check plumb, using a level placed on two adjacent sides of each post; secure the post position with temporary wood braces nailed to wood stakes driven into the ground.

Beam

Post cap

3 Attach beams and rafters
Position a beam on top of the posts that will support it. Check that the post is vertical and the beam level, and adjust if necessary. Nail the post caps to the beam. Set and space rafters on tops of the beams and secure them with framing anchors.

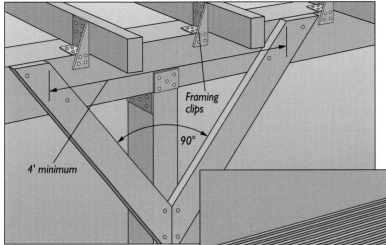

Framing clips

90°

4' minimum

4 Bracing the overhead
Nail or bolt 1x4 or 1x6 braces with ends cut at 45° between beams and posts. Cut the knee braces long enough so that the beam ends are at least 2' from the post caps. Remove temporary post braces.

5 Covering your structure
Cover the rafters with lath, 1x2s, or 2x2s, spaced to achieve the desired amount of shading. For additional roofing ideas, see page 91.

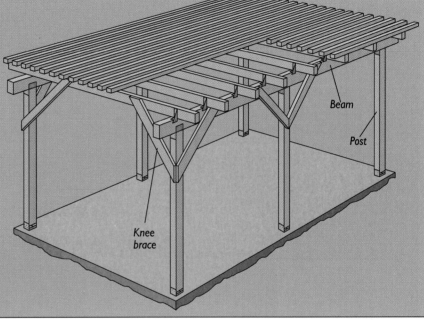

Beam

Post

Knee brace

Post Anchor Options

When building an overhead above an existing concrete patio, posts can be set in post anchors fastened to the patio with expansion bolts (*above, right*). This requires drilling holes into the patio with a masonry bit.

For existing patios paved with masonry units, it is often easiest to install precast pier blocks, leveled in both directions, on footings just outside the edge of the patio (*below right*). Otherwise, part of the patio must be pulled up to make room for the footings and piers.

Footings should extend 6 inches below the local frostline, to avoid heaving caused by freezing and thawing.

Prepunched holes for nails

Post

Metal post anchor

Existing slab

Expanding anchor bolt

Pier block

LEDGER

Some overheads rely on the use of a ledger to support one end of the rafters at the house. The ledger must be fastened to a masonry wall or to the framing of a wood frame house. If you have a one-story house, you'll fasten the ledger to wall studs, or if the overhead falls just under the house roof, you can attach the ledger to the roof rafters. On a two-story house, you can attach the ledger to the floor framing as shown below. Locate the middle of the ledger about 6 inches below the interior floor level. To transfer this measurement to the exterior wall, use a window or door sill as a reference point.

Securing the ledger: Fasten the ledger to the house as you would a deck ledger. First you'll need to brace or nail the ledger temporarily at the desired height; make sure it's perfectly level. For a wood frame house, drill lag screw holes into the framing every 16 inches as shown and screw the ledger in place with ⅜-inch lag screws and flat washers. For a masonry wall, use expanding anchor bolts at the same intervals.

Keeping the rain at bay: Unless the ledger is protected from the rain by the eaves or by its own solid cover material and flashing, you'll have to prevent water from accumulating in the joint between the ledger and the house. To do this, space the ledger out from the wall with flat washers. Or you can protect the ledger with aluminum or galvanized sheet metal Z-flashing.

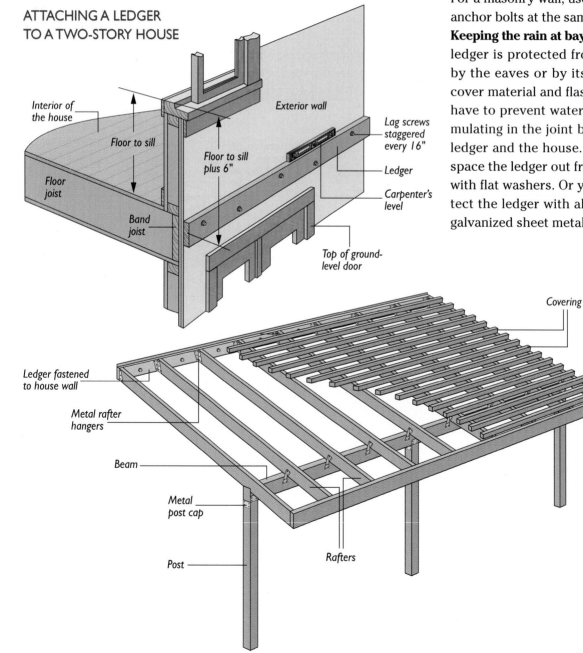

ATTACHING A LEDGER
TO A TWO-STORY HOUSE

Interior of the house

Floor to sill

Floor joist

Band joist

Exterior wall

Floor to sill plus 6"

Top of ground-level door

Lag screws staggered every 16"

Ledger

Carpenter's level

Covering

Ledger fastened to house wall

Metal rafter hangers

Beam

Metal post cap

Post

Rafters

Once you've erected the overhead structure of posts, beams, and rafters, you need just to add the finishing touch: a cover material. When you select roofing material, be sure the material you choose will create the environment you want. One material may turn your patio into an oven because of restricted air circulation. Another may provide welcome shade in summer, only to darken an otherwise sunny space in winter.

Overhead covers come in two types: open or solid. Generally, open style covers are made from wood of various dimensions. Several solid materials are shown below. Lightweight materials, such as fabrics, are versatile as they allow the overhead cover to be removed before the arrival of winter, opening the patio to sunlight when it is needed the most. Home improvement centers can provide you with material suitable for your home's climate and appearance.

A GALLERY OF OVERHEAD COVERS

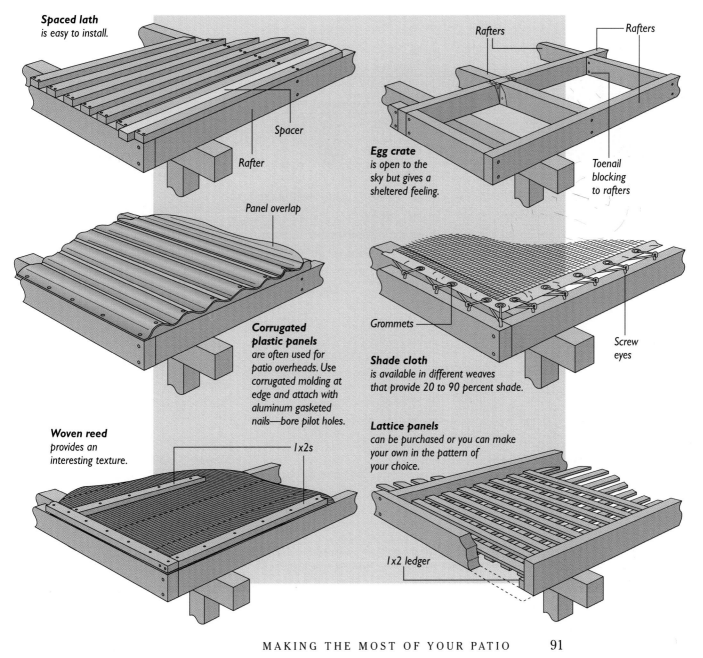

Spaced lath is easy to install.

Spacer

Rafter

Rafters

Rafters

Egg crate is open to the sky but gives a sheltered feeling.

Toenail blocking to rafters

Panel overlap

Corrugated plastic panels are often used for patio overheads. Use corrugated molding at edge and attach with aluminum gasketed nails—bore pilot holes.

Grommets

Shade cloth is available in different weaves that provide 20 to 90 percent shade.

Screw eyes

Woven reed provides an interesting texture.

1x2s

Lattice panels can be purchased or you can make your own in the pattern of your choice.

1x2 ledger

Fences for Shelter and Privacy

Fences can shelter a patio from the elements, define the area, and provide privacy, transforming the space into a secure, attractive, and comfortable retreat from the outside world.

To increase seclusion and wind protection, look to a closed design, such as solid board, face panel, or grapestake fencing. When you want to break up a blank expanse of fencing—in a solid panel fence, for example—a simple oval or square window or cutout, especially when framing a view, lends a sense of mystery and discovery. Shrubs planted along the fence also soften the look of solid fencing.

If you are looking for some degree of privacy but don't want to compromise ventilation, vertical lath or lattice is a good choice, as long as the space doesn't require complete protection.

Vines trained onto lattice trellises or wire frames can block wind and sun, without destroying the airy, open feeling of your patio. (Remember to choose attractive plants that don't attract bees or other insects.)

Sheared evergreen hedges give a patio a sense of closure. Higher hedges, especially dense ones, make very good insulators against street noise.

Capped with narrow lattice panels, a solid board fence produces near-complete privacy while remaining an attractive design element.

COMMON FENCE STYLES

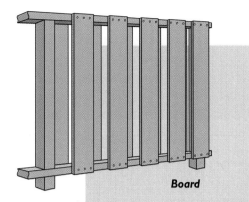

Board

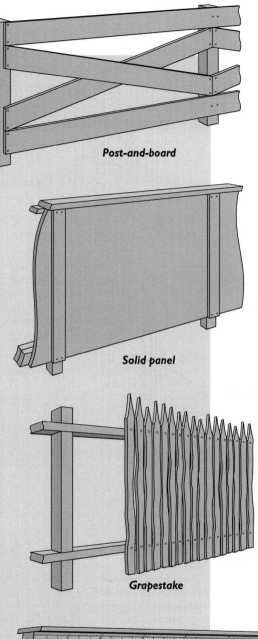

Post-and-board

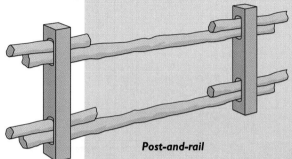

Post-and-rail

Solid panel

Picket

Grapestake

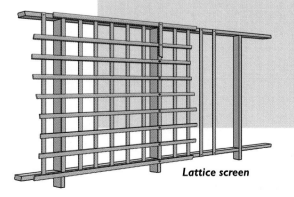

Lattice screen

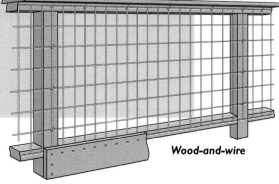

Wood-and-wire

Warming Up

To get the most possible use out of your patio, you may want to consider adding some type of heating device to take the edge off the cold.

With a patio heater, or a fire pit, you can enjoy patio living on cool nights and mornings. Freestanding heaters and more permanent, mounted units are both available.

For heating units to perform well, they need to be in the right location. Pick an intimate spot. If you heat near a wall or other solid structure, the heat will radiate back into your space. The ideal location contains a combination of walls, fences, and overhead structures that will prevent the wind from counteracting the warmth.

Fire pits, or even portable barbecues, are good sources of heat. Low, round metal braziers are an inexpensive and convenient option that allow you to move the heat to various locations on the patio.

Portable pottery fire pits generate generous amounts of heat from a small fire. But use them cautiously: they're lightweight and reasonably fragile, and they may break if the fire inside is too hot. You'll get the best results from burning kindling-size wood.

Remember that any open fire is a potential hazard. Be sure your fire is well away from tree branches, patio overheads, or anything else that could be ignited by flying sparks. In some places, a permit is needed for any outdoor fire, so call your fire department first and ask about local regulations.

Sitting around the campfire has never been so comfortable and convenient. A slump-block fire pit is the focal point of this modular patio design that includes a matching low wall.

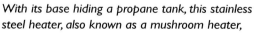

Mushroom heater
With its base hiding a propane tank, this stainless steel heater, also known as a mushroom heater, provides a comfort zone 12 to 15 feet in diameter. Mushroom heaters are the most powerful outdoor heaters in terms of energy output, but some of the heat radiates vertically, above the desired area. They must be put away when not in use as bugs, moisture, chlorine, and salt air can affect their performance.

Cooling Off

If blistering summertime heat is keeping you off the patio, you can benefit from a plan that incorporates one or more of the following cooling methods.

Cooling with water: Although garden pools, fountains, and waterfalls often appear in dry-climate patio schemes for esthetic reasons, water from such sources also adds moisture to the air and helps lower the temperature on hot summer days.

For a more pronounced effect, consider installing a mister. Misters are usually easy to install, and because they use a minimum of water (some only three gallons an hour) they can be operated constantly without drainage problems.

Cooling with plants: Shading with shrubs, trees, and vines may be your best solution to summer heat. Exposed to the sun, plant foliage absorbs, reflects, and reradiates heat efficiently without over-heating the area it protects. If you live in a mild climate, the filtered shade of a birch or olive tree may be enough; in hotter climates you may need the denser foliage of a fruitless mulberry or sycamore. Be sure, however, that the plants you choose are not so dense that they block essential air movement.

Cooling with air circulation: Ensuring the free circulation of air is another effective defense against summer heat, especially in hot, humid climates. If you're fortunate enough to have a prevailing summer breeze, plan trees, shrubs, and fences to facilitate its passage across your patio. If summer air is still, keep shelter structures open to avoid creating a heat trap. Hanging outdoor fans add both air movement and a decorative touch to an outdoor space.

A lattice-covered overhead, equipped with a misting system, shades and waters a jungle of ferns. In a dry climate, misting systems can lower patio temperatures by up to 20 degrees in just minutes.

Patio Furniture

Patio furniture will likely get a lot of use, so make comfort a priority when selecting new pieces. Consider its durability as well, since you don't want to keep replacing furniture when it becomes weathered or weak. Most standard garden furniture is made of aluminum, wrought iron, plastic, resin composites, or wood. Folding furniture stores easily, but tends not to be as durable. Wood furniture, though weighty, has a timeless appeal; it's also long lasting, provided it is made of durable wood and weather-proofed. Wood and wicker should be stored inside during winter. Built-in perimeter benches provide permanent seating that is particularly useful where space is tight. The photos here show functional yet durable options.

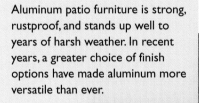

Aluminum patio furniture is strong, rustproof, and stands up well to years of harsh weather. In recent years, a greater choice of finish options have made aluminum more versatile than ever.

Naturally finished, hand-woven wicker has a light, summery appeal and stays cool and comfortable in hot weather. The bamboo framing gives this set a tropical look.

Hand-forged wrought aluminum frames and vinyl strap seating create furniture that is not only durable and modestly priced, but also very comfortable.

Resin furniture (made from polypropylene plastic) is extremely economical. Available in an ever-increasing number of styles, it stays cool in the sun and requires little maintenance. Chairs often nest for off-season storage.

Classic wrought iron furniture—with its attention to detail—offers a distinctive, formal look that has long been a patio favorite.

CHOOSING WOOD

Outdoor furniture made of wood has an enduring appeal not matched by other more practical cast resin or metal counterparts. However, if you choose wooden furniture for your backyard, it must be more than simply inviting and comfortable, it must be rugged enough to survive outside. Outdoor furniture is typically subject to relatively harsh conditions, but with appropriate materials, design, joinery, hardware, and finishing, you can purchase or build outdoor furniture that's long lasting and attractive. If you decide to build, the first step is choosing the right wood.

Outdoor woods: Different woods give different feels, looks, and textures. Some combine strength and resistance but are expensive and difficult to work with for most people. Others are less expensive and easy to work with but are relatively weak and prone to decay. Good compromises include cedar and white oak, which are relatively long lasting but not too expensive. Start by selecting pieces that are straight and flat, not bowed, warped, or twisted in any way. For the best quality, look for the highest grade lumber you can afford. If you plan to finish your pieces, your lumber needn't be perfect—you may be able to use grades with small, tight knots.

These two classic outdoor furniture designs show off wood's versatility and charm. The heavy teak pieces (*left*) have an understated formality, while the variations on the Adirondack chair (*below*), bring to mind sunny summers and times gone by.

Wood finishing: Water and sunlight are your furniture's worst enemies. Penetrating oils, varnishes, and paints are the finishes most often chosen to prevent water damage. Paint offers the most protection from the sun. Generally, the higher the gloss the greater the sun protection. Some varnishes, such as spar varnish, contain (UV) filters that protect the wood from the sun.

Furniture built from decay-resistant woods, such as redwood or cedar heartwood, may be left unfinished. They turn gray over time but require little maintenance other than scrubbing away dirt and mildew. Exposure can cause these woods to crack, however. To protect them and prevent graying and mildew, use a clear water repellent with UV protectors and a mildewcide. If you pre-

fer the natural gray color, use a product with no UV protectors.

If you choose a less decay-resistant wood, finishing is vital to protect and beautify it. Finishing keeps insects from eating your furniture. And a colored topcoat will conceal mismatched grain.

The most common choices in finishes are shown below along with their advantages and disadvantages.

CHARACTERISTICS OF COMMON OUTDOOR FINISHES

TYPE	ADVANTAGES	DISADVANTAGES	GENERAL TRAITS
CLEAR FINISHES			
Penetrating resin	Easiest to apply. Gives a natural, no-finish look.	Provides little surface protection.	Soaks into wood pores and darkens the wood grain.
Polyurethane	Simple to brush on. It's tough, alcohol-, heat-, and water-resistant.	Slow-drying. You can't coat other finishes with it.	Protects with a thick coating, and enhances the grain with a slight darkening effect.
Varnish	Seals and protects with 4 to 5 coats	Tends to yellow with age.	Shaking it creates bubbles, which may mar the finish.
STAINS			
Pigmented oil stain	Simple to wipe on and off with a rag, it's useful for changing and matching wood colors.	Often obscures pores and grain.	Colors don't fade or bleed, and are available ready-mixed in a wide variety of hues.
Penetrating oil stain	Similar to a penetrating resin, but with color; pores and grains show.	Penetrates irregularly on softwoods and plywoods; not good for matching colors.	Soaks into wood, and colors by means of dyes, not pigments.
Water stain	Bright, clear, and permanent. Thins easily and cleans up with water.	Water swells the fibers, so you need to resand; slow drying, hard to apply.	Comes in a powdered-mix form, dyeing the wood.
PAINTS			
Oil-base enamel	Durable, washable; good adhesion and coverage.	Slow-drying.	All gloss, semigloss, and flat colors totally conceal the grain.
Latex enamel	Thinned and cleaned with water; is quick-drying.	Slightly less coverage than oil-based.	All semigloss and flat colors are available. Completely conceals grain.
CLEAR WATER REPELLENTS			
	Do not color wood; seal and protect with one coat.	Require yearly reapplication; cause wood to darken slightly.	Also known as water sealers; cause water to bead on surface of wood.

Lawn Chair

Few pieces of outdoor furniture offer both the comfort and distinctive look of a traditional Adirondack lawn chair. With its tall, tilted backrest and a reclining seat, it offers an inviting and relaxing place to sit, while its wide armrests provide enough surface for a few magazines or a refreshing drink.

CUT OUT THE PATTERNS

Use the grid patterns on the opposite page as a guide to cut out arm

pieces (A and B) and seat legs (D) from 1-by-6s. The cutting list, also shown opposite, gives the dimensions of the arms and legs as well as the other pieces of the chair. For the tapering outside back slats (G), rip and sand a 32-inch 1-by-3 into two identical pieces, with ends measuring ½ and 1⅞ inches wide.

START AT THE FRONT

Cut a ¾-inch-deep by 3½-inch-long dado in each front leg (E), starting 10½ inches up from the bottom. Attach the arm supports (B) so

FINISHING UP

Once the chair has been assembled, it can be painted, stained, or left to its natural wood color. If you choose not to paint it, protect the wood against the elements with a nontoxic water-repellent preservative.
Design: William Crosby.

The chair is held together with waterproof glue and galvanized screws. Predrill and countersink all screw holes before assembling the chair. Here, the maneuverability of a cordless drill makes the job easier.

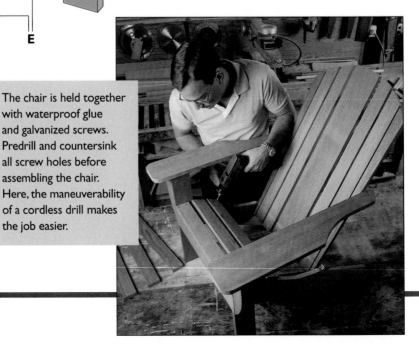

they're flush with the top and front edges of the legs, then attach support blocks (C) flush with the tops of the legs behind the arm supports. Attach the front stretcher (F) between the front legs; the stretcher should sit flush in the dado. Secure seat legs (D) to the front legs so they butt against the back of stretcher (F) and are flush with the top edge.

SEAT AND BACK

Mount the center back slat (H) on the wide side of the 1-by-3 bottom cross brace (I), making sure the bottoms are flush. Attach two inside full slats (J) ⅝ inch from each side of H, then attach the outside full slats (K) ⅜ inch from the J pieces. Screw the ½-inch end of each of the G slats to the brace, spacing them ¼ inch from the adjacent slats. Center and screw in the upper cross brace (L) so its bottom is 27½ inches up from the

bottom of the back slats. Rip a 30° bevel along the top edge of the middle cross brace (M), then mount M 15½ inches up from the bottom of the back slats. Use a string extending to 14 inches below the top of the H slat to trace an arc in the chair back, then cut out the arc.

ATTACHING THE UNITS

Attach the 1-by-3 back brace (N) on the seat legs. Tuck the seat back's brace (I) under N, then screw the legs to the brace. Position the arms so they overhang the front of the supports (B) by 3 inches and the inner edges of the front legs by ¼ inch, then screw the support blocks (C) to the arms. Use single screws to attach the arms to the end of the brace (M), making sure they're even with one another. Screw the seat legs (D) into the brace (I); then attach the N brace to the I

brace with four screws. Finally, attach the six 1-by-3 slats (O) ½ inch apart so the front edge of the first one is flush with the front of the stretcher.

CUTTING AND MATERIALS LIST		
A	Arm	Two 1x6s @ 28½"
B	Arm support	Two 1x6s @ 10½"
C	Support block	Two 1x3s @ 3½"
D	Seat leg	Two 1x6s @ 31½"
E	Front leg	Two 1x4s @ 21"
F	Front stretcher	One 1x4 @ 23"
G	Tapering back slat	Two 1x3s @ 32"
H	Center back slat	One 1x6 @ 35"
I	Bottom cross brace	One 1x3 @ 20"
J	Inside full slat	Two 1x3s @ 35"
K	Outside full slat	Two 1x3s @ 34"
L	Upper cross brace	One 1x2 @ 21"
M	Middle cross brace	One 1x2 @ 24"
N	Back and leg brace	One 1x3 @ 21½"
O	Seat slats	Six 1x3s @ 21½"
	Galvanized flathead wood screws	1¼"x#8 (1 box)
	Waterproof glue	
	Finishing materials	

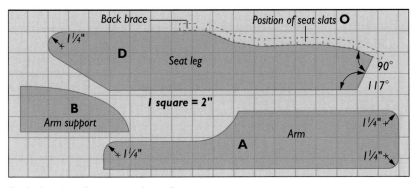

Scale drawings for arms and seat legs
In the scale drawing above, 1 square equals 2 inches. Simply enlarge the grid to produce the right-size patterns for cutting out the arms and seat legs.

Redwood Garden Table

Designed to stand up to the elements, this small redwood coffee table is perfect for casual outdoor meals. You can also play board games on it or use it to display flowers and plants. When not in use, the table disassembles for easy, minimum-space storage. The removable top, made from 1-by-3s, lifts off; the two halves of the base slide apart.

GETTING STARTED

Begin by cutting all the wooden parts to length according to the cutting list. Be sure to mark and check all cuts with a square.

CUTTING SLOTS IN BASE

Mark and cut the slots in (B), as shown in *Diagram 2*. Be sure to

cut on the waste side of the cutting lines. Cut carefully; if the slots are too deep or too shallow, the base won't fit together properly. (It's better to cut too little rather than too much—you can always remove more, but adding wood is another story.) Sand or file the slots smooth, then fit the pieces together to check for proper depth of slots.

ASSEMBLING BASE

Mark hole placement on the cross pieces, as shown in Diagram 4. Drill $7/8$"-diameter holes $3/8$" deep. Sandwich a leg between two cross-pieces, making sure the ends are flush and that the pieces are positioned at a 90° angle (use a square to check). Clamp the pieces—placing a piece of scrap wood under the jaws of the clamps to protect the soft redwood from damage. Centering a $1/4$" bit in the $7/8$"-diameter holes, drill bolt holes through

REDWOOD GARDEN TABLE

This versatile outdoor table is easy to build, making it a good project for the less experienced do-it-yourselfer. Redwood is an ideal material for outdoor use. Pressure-treated wood is not appropriate for table-top use, as it contains potentially harmful chemicals.

all three pieces. Put a washer on one bolt, push the bolt through the hole, add another washer and tighten on a nut. Repeat for all bolt holes. Fit together the two halves to form the complete base *(see Diagram 2)*.

ASSEMBLING TABLE TOP

Leaving a ⅛" space between top slats to allow for wood movement, make sure all the top slats (C) fit properly. Then screw all the slats to the two perpendicular (C) frame pieces, making sure

the corners are 90° and keeping all top slats parallel. Then add (D). Sand the wood, slightly rounding the edges and corners, and apply two coats of clear polyurethane finish. When dry, set the top on the base.

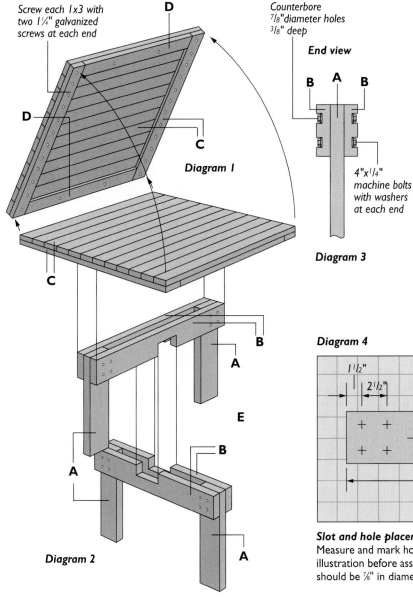

Screw each 1x3 with two 1¼" galvanized screws at each end

Diagram 1

Diagram 2

Counterbore ⅞"diameter holes ³⁄₈" deep

End view

4"x¼" machine bolts with washers at each end

Diagram 3

CUTTING AND MATERIALS LIST		
A	**Legs**	Four 2x6s @ 16¾"
B	**Crosspieces**	Four 2x6s @ 25"
C	**Top slats**	Fourteen 1x3s @ 30"
D	**Two 1x3s**	Two 1x3s @ 25"
Screws		Sixty 1¼"
Machine bolts		16 @ ¼"x4" with nuts
Washers		32 @ ¼"
Waterproof glue		
Clear polyurethane exterior finish		
(All hardware and fasteners should be rust-resistant.)		

Diagram 4

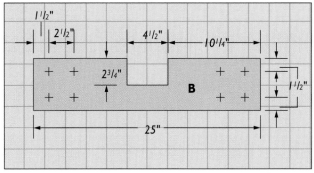

1½" 2½" 4½" 10¼" 2¾" B 1½" 25"

Slot and hole placements

Measure and mark hole placements as shown in the above illustration before assembling the two halves of the base. Holes should be ⅞" in diameter and ⅜" deep.

Barbecues

Barbecues range from classic masonry structures to permanent or portable manufactured units. Whatever style you choose, be sure to plan enough working space beside the grill for dishes, pans, and barbecue accessories.

Built-in units: Today's sophisticated masonry units are likely to incorporate built-in smokers, commercial woks, and pizza ovens, along with the traditional grill. The focal point for outdoor entertaining, these barbecues are big, bold, permanent structures designed for dedicated backyard chefs. Plan the location of the built-in carefully. Ideally, the unit should be close to the kitchen and sheltered from the weather. Most communities have strict ordinances about outdoor fires. Check with your local fire department and building inspection department before you or your contractor begin work on a permanent unit.

Charcoal-fired barbecues: The most popular models are open braziers, covered kettles, and boxes with lids.

Open braziers vary from table-top units to large, freestanding models. Most braziers feature a cooking grill that can be raised or lowered to adjust the distance between firebed and food, thus controlling the heat.

Covered kettles and boxes with hinged lids can be used either covered for indirect heat—to cook larger cuts of meat, such as roasts or turkeys—or open for more traditional direct heat grilling.

Gas and electric barbecues: Barbecues powered by electricity or

Outdoor cooking and entertaining is the chief focus of this patio. An attractive curved counter has a built-in grill. The overhead provides shelter from the midday sun to ensure comfortable lunch-time dining.

gas provide two alternatives to charcoal-fired barbecues. Models using natural or bottled gas include kettles and single or double box-shaped units; barbecues heated by electric coils are available in a similar range of styles.

Outdoor units fueled by bottled gas usually roll on wheels; natural gas units are mounted on a fixed pedestal and need to be connected to a gas line. Electric units can simply be plugged into a GFCI outlet. All gas and some electric models use a briquet-shaped material such as lava rock above the burner.

Features such as smokers, auxiliary burners, and rotisseries pro-vide extra flexibility when bar-becuing. Smokers, for example, can be used merely to add smoke fla-voring to grilled food, or can be designed to cold smoke food. Gas barbecues often have the same capabilities as gas ranges, allowing for easy preparation of sauces and other dishes outside.

GRILL INSTALLATION

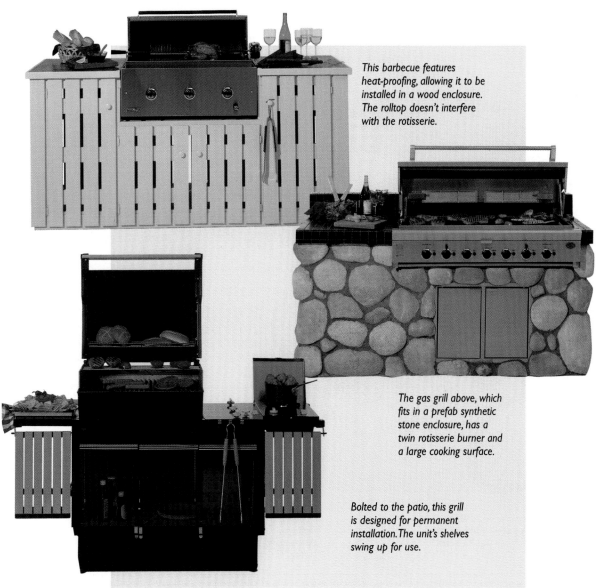

This barbecue features heat-proofing, allowing it to be installed in a wood enclosure. The rolltop doesn't interfere with the rotisserie.

The gas grill above, which fits in a prefab synthetic stone enclosure, has a twin rotisserie burner and a large cooking surface.

Bolted to the patio, this grill is designed for permanent installation. The unit's shelves swing up for use.

Serving Cart

Outdoor entertaining doesn't have to involve making trip after trip into the house to retrieve items from the kitchen. With this serving cart you can transport everything you need in short order and in style. Attractive and simple to build, it makes patio life a lot easier.

MAKING THE FIRST CUTS

Begin by cutting the pieces to length according to the cutting list on the opposite page. Then, use a table saw to rip each leg (A) and top frame piece (B) so that they are exactly 2⅜ inches wide. At the edge opposite the ripped side of the B pieces, and along one edge of the bottom frame pieces (C), rabbet a one-inch by one-inch

groove, as shown in Drawing 3. Then cut a ¾-inch-wide by ½-inch-deep dado in each leg, 1½ inches from the end. The bottom end slats (G) should fit into the dadoes *(see Diagram 2)*.

THE LEGS AND FRAME ASSEMBLY

Counterbore ¾-inch-diameter holes ⅜ inch deep in A and B, as shown in Drawing 1, for the lag screws. Center a ¼-inch bit in these holes and drill clearance

Diagram 1

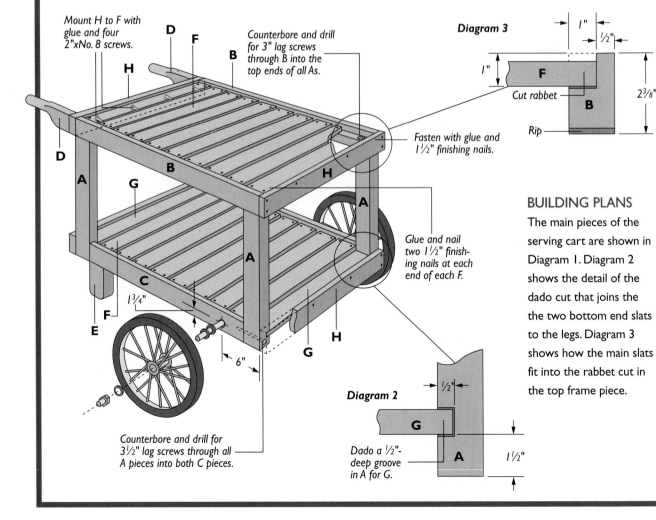

Mount H to F with glue and four 2"xNo. 8 screws.

Counterbore and drill for 3" lag screws through B into the top ends of all As.

Fasten with glue and 1½" finishing nails.

Glue and nail two 1½" finishing nails at each end of each F.

Counterbore and drill for 3½" lag screws through all A pieces into both C pieces.

Diagram 3

Cut rabbet

Rip

Diagram 2

Dado a ½"-deep groove in A for G.

BUILDING PLANS

The main pieces of the serving cart are shown in Diagram 1. Diagram 2 shows the detail of the dado cut that joins the the two bottom end slats to the legs. Diagram 3 shows how the main slats fit into the rabbet cut in the top frame piece.

holes through B into A and through A into C. Finish drilling pilot holes in the ends of A and C with a ⁵⁄₃₂-inch bit. Glue and screw the pieces together, slipping a washer onto each lag screw. Let the glue dry, then sand the frames. Stand them up and fit the G pieces into the dadoes in the legs. Space the main slats (F) evenly, about ½ inch apart, along the rabbeted

edges of B and C. Glue and nail them in place with 1½-inch finishing nails, then set the nails. Cut the end frame pieces (H) to match the widths of B and C *(see Diagram 1)*.

CUTTING THE HANDLES

Use a saber saw to rough-cut the handles to the shape shown in the drawing below; smooth them with a rasp, then sand. Glue and screw the handles flush to each end of one of the H pieces, first drilling pilot holes for countersinking 2¾-inch No. 14 screws. Glue and screw that H piece to one end of the top of the cart, first drilling pilot holes for countersinking 2-inch No. 8 screws into the edge of the slat (F). Glue and nail the remaining H pieces, using 1½-inch finishing nails. Sand all the surfaces and fill any holes with wood filler. Sand again and seal with one coat of polyurethane penetrating oil-sealer finish.

MOUNTING THE WHEELS

Drill ⁷⁄₁₆-inch holes for the axle in both C pieces, as shown in Drawing 1. Push the axle through both holes in the cart. On one side, slip two washers on the axle, then a wheel, another washer, and a hub nut. Measure the distance from C to the end of the hub nut. On the other side, mark the axle at that distance plus ⅛ inch, use a hacksaw to cut off any excess axle, then attach the other wheel.

ATTACHING THE BOTTOM LEGS

With the cart level, measure from the bottom of C to the ground; add 1½ inches (the total should be 6¾ inches). Round the corners at one end of each bottom leg (E). Drill pilot holes through the bottom end slats and the end frames into E for 2¼-inch No. 14 screws. Screw through G from the top and through H from one end to attach the legs.

	CUTTING AND MATERIALS LIST	
A	**Legs**	Four 2x3s @ 20"
B	**Top side frame**	Two 2x3s @ 29½"
C	**Bottom side frame**	Two 2x3s @ 24¾"
D	**Handles**	Two 2x3s @ 9"
E	**Bottom leg**	Two 2x3s @ 6¾"
F	**Main slats**	Eighteen 1x3s @ 20"
G	**Bottom end slats**	Two 1x3s @ 19"
H	**End frames**	Four 1x3s @ 21"
Galvanized lag screws		Four @ 2"xNo. 8 Four @ ¼"x3" Four @ ¼"x3½"
Galvanized flathead screws		Four @ 2¾"xNo. 14 Four @ 2¼"xNo. 14
1½" galvanized finishing nails		½ pound
Rubber wheels		Two @ 12" diameter
Steel rod		30" long @ ⁷⁄₁₆"
Waterproof glue		
Wood filler		
Polyurethane penetrating oil-sealer finish		

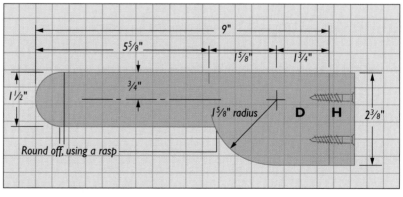

Cutting detail for the handles
The drawing above shows the cutting detail for the serving cart handles. Follow the measurements closely to shape a pair of handles for your project. Remember that the initial cutting doesn't have to be precise, a wood rasp and sandpaper will take care of any imperfections.

Patio Water Features

Adding a splash of water to a patio setting—with a tub garden, birdbath, or fountain—creates an eye-catching focal point and brings energy and charm to the space.

TUB GARDENS

With nothing more than a water-filled tub placed in a sunny spot you can quickly and easily introduce the appeal of a water garden.

The container: Searching for the right container is half the fun of tub gardening. Any size will do, but to house a standard water lily or lotus, you'll need a container at least 18 inches across; a 25 gallon container is a good bet. Dwarf lilies are great for smaller containers, or try a selection of grasses with different foliage colors and textures. And you can always hide the main container in a more attractive—but less watertight—barrel or tub. Examples of commercial and recycled tub gardens are shown on the opposite page.

Before putting a container in place, line it with a flexible pond liner (PVC or EPDM). With the exception of plants that float free on the water surface, root aquatic plants before placing them in water. Most water gardeners prefer to use movable plastic containers that allow you to rearrange plants easily within the tub. These tend to be perforated to allow roots to better obtain nourishment. Solid containers will stunt growth; this can be useful to control the growth of a plant that threatens to monopolize the container.

The plants: With the recent boom in water gardening, finding plants for a tub garden is much easier than it once was. Nowadays, even general garden centers often sell suitable plants. A greater selection is available through the mail from specialty companies. Before you place an order, ask how the plants will be delivered. Some suppliers ship plants in tiny plastic contain-

An old-fashioned hand pump is the perfect complement to a barrel pond. Of course, no hand pumping is required; a submersible pump keeps the water moving.

ers, which helps ensure they are kept damp (however, the added weight can increase shipping costs).

Use high-grade potting soil without organic amendments. Avoid sandy or limestone-rich earth, and don't use peat composts, as they will float out of containers and increase the acidity of the water. Generic fertilizers and manure should also be avoided, as they tend to cloud and pollute the water.

Finally, choose a sunny patio spot—most aquatic plants need four to six hours of sunlight a day.

TUB GARDEN CONTAINERS

Almost anything capable of holding water can—with suitable cleaning, appropriate placement, and a little imagination—become an attractive garden accent pond. Make a tiny tub garden in a bonsai pot. Or give an old claw-footed bathtub new life with a couple of delicately scented lilies and some slender grasses.

Old wooden trough
Found at an auction or in grandpa's shed, an old trough can make a charming garden, as long as you use a water-tight liner.

New watering trough
You can buy a new metal trough, either oblong or round and holding about 170 gallons, at a feed-and-grain store.

Wooden half barrel
Used barrels should be scrubbed clean and lined, both for watertightness and to prevent any substances in the wood from leaching into the water. Smaller rocks and pebbles added after planting will hide the tops of pots.

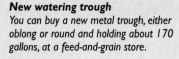

Cast-iron kettle
An old soup kettle may be just the thing for your patio. If it has no feet, you can support it on crossed wooden blocks cut to shape.

Terra-cotta planter
Be sure to plug the drain hole or add a pond liner before planting. Add a bed of gravel to raise plants to the right height.

GARDEN FOUNTAINS AND POOLS

Adding moving water to your patio environment introduces a cooling effect and provides a soothing barrier against unwanted outside noise. Even if heat and noise aren't problems, you may still want to include a garden pool or fountain simply for esthetic reasons.

If you decide to add a garden pool to your landscape, consult a landscape professional for design ideas.
Fountains: Water in motion is nearly always dramatic, and the simplest fountain can add a musical dimension to the smallest patio.

Garden fountains usually fall into one of three categories: Spray fountains are made versatile by assorted fountain heads that send water upward in shapes ranging from massive columns to lacy mists. Spill (or wall) fountains send a single stream of water falling into a pool or series of tiered pans or shelves. Splash fountains, which are almost always professionally designed, force water up through a piece of sculpture.

Garden pools: The size and shape of a garden pool is limited only by your imagination and your space. A still-water garden pool can be small and decorative or complex and natural, depending on the effect you want to achieve. For the do-it-yourselfer, the only rule is this: Keep it simple. Complex designs are difficult to build and rarely successful.

In an unusual twist on the garden fountain, water pours from a concrete block and stucco wall beside the patio. The steep fountain ramp is lined with Saltillo pavers. Water is recycled with a recirculating pump. *Landscape architect: Deweese/Burton Associates.*

Spas and hot tubs are a popular garden feature. Not only do they provide an invigorating alfresco bath, they double as a decorative water feature.

Once you have decided to add a spa or tub to your patio, you're faced with numerous design decisions. For help, look through home improvement magazines, visit the homes of friends who have spas or hot tubs, or consult a local spa or hot tub dealer.

Spas and hot tubs differ principally in material and form, not function. Prefab units made from fiberglass or acrylic are available in many shapes. Gunite spas, made with a mix of hydrated cement and aggregate, can be shaped as desired. Spas must be set in sand, which in turn is held in place by stable earth. Custom-built concrete spas are usually included as adjuncts to swimming pools and are built at the same time as the pool.

Hot tubs are made of wood in the manner of large, usually straight-sided barrels. With the proper foundation, tubs are self-supporting, making them a good option above ground. They are relatively inexpensive to install.

Portable spas can be added easily above grade. You can also set your spa into the patio, so it lies flush with the surface, though this will require additional excavation and more involved installation.

A border of used brick surrounds the spa, tying it into the patio design, while a scattering of natural boulders adds visual interest and a modicum of privacy.

Patio Lighting

Good outdoor lighting is both functional and esthetic. On the practical side it will give you the right kind of light when you need it for entertaining, outdoor cooking, or a lively evening volleyball game. And it can add to the beauty of your outdoor space by highlighting architectural elements and garden plantings.

Thoughtful planning is the key to effective lighting. First, decide how much light you need. If you want casual evening conversation, soft and indirect illumination will give you enough light to see without robbing the evening of its mood. If you're an outdoor chef, you will need a bright light for the barbecue area. To light outdoor games, you will need high-intensity illumination.

Low or standard voltage? A low voltage lighting system is often used outdoors because it is energy efficient, safe, and easy to install. See page 113 for installation overview. The standard 120-volt system still has the advantage of projecting more light as well as having outlets that accept standard power tools and patio heaters.

Fixtures and bulbs: Useful outdoor fixtures include well lights and other portable uplights for accenting or silhouetting foliage, spread lights for illuminating paths or bridges, and downlights for pinpointing spe-

The diffused lighting of this patio is achieved by directing low-level lights against the garden fence. Softer lights, mounted on the wall under the overhang, add to the warm ambiance.

cial garden features. See page 115 for illustrations.

Most outdoor systems are made of bronze, cast or extruded aluminum, copper, or plastic, but you can also find decorative stone, concrete, and wood fixtures (redwood, cedar, and teak weather best). Size varies. When evaluating fixtures, look for gaskets, high-quality components at joints and pivot points, and locking devices for pointing the fixture in one direction.

Choose the effect and bulb you want first, and then the appropri-

Adding a 12-Volt System

To install a low-voltage system for outdoor use, you'll need a transformer, usually housed in a weatherproof box, to step the household current of 120 volts down to 12 volts. Mount the transformer near the weatherproof switch or receptacle and then run a cable a few inches below the ground from the low-voltage side of the transformer to the desired locations for your lights. Some fixtures simply clip onto the wire, while others must be wired into the system. Some low-voltage lights come in a kit with a transformer. Be sure to use the correct wire size specified in the instructions. If you don't already have an outlet to plug the transformer into, have an electrician install a GFCI-protected outdoor outlet (*below*).

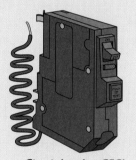

GFCI receptacle
According to current electrical codes, any new outside receptacle must be protected by a ground fault circuit interrupter (GFCI, or GFI). Whenever the amounts of incoming and outgoing current are not equal—indicating current leakage (a "ground fault")—the GFCI opens the circuit instantly, cutting off the power.

Circuit breaker GFCI

Receptacle GFCI

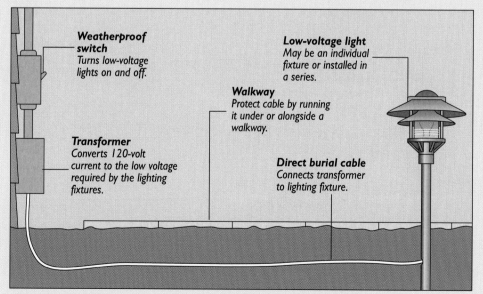

A typical 12-volt installation
Since a 12-volt system uses a greatly reduced voltage, special conduit and boxes of other outdoor wiring are not required. Most transformers are rated for home use from 100 to 300 watts. The higher the rating, the more lengths of 100-foot cable—and consequently the more light fixtures—can be connected to the transformer. Most transformers are encased in weatherproof boxes; to be safe, though, plan to install yours at least a foot off the ground in a sheltered location.

Weatherproof switch
Turns low-voltage lights on and off.

Transformer
Converts 120-volt current to the low voltage required by the lighting fixtures.

Low-voltage light
May be an individual fixture or installed in a series.

Walkway
Protect cable by running it under or alongside a walkway.

Direct burial cable
Connects transformer to lighting fixture.

ate fixtures. Low-value halogen MR-16 bulbs are perfect for accenting; PAR spotlights, available in both low and standard voltage, are best to light trees or wide areas. Today's fluorescent lights are popular for outdoor use; both their shape and their color rendition are superior to older types.

Avoiding glare: Because the contrast between darkness and a light source is so great, glare can be a big problem at night. Keep the following points in mind when you're planning your outdoor lighting system.

Use shielded fixtures: With a shielded light fixture, the bulb area is completely hidden by an opaque covering that directs the light away from the viewer's eyes. Instead of a bright spot of light, the eye sees the warm glow of the lighted object.

Place fixtures out of sight lines: By placing fixtures either close to the ground (along a walk), or very high, you can direct them in such a

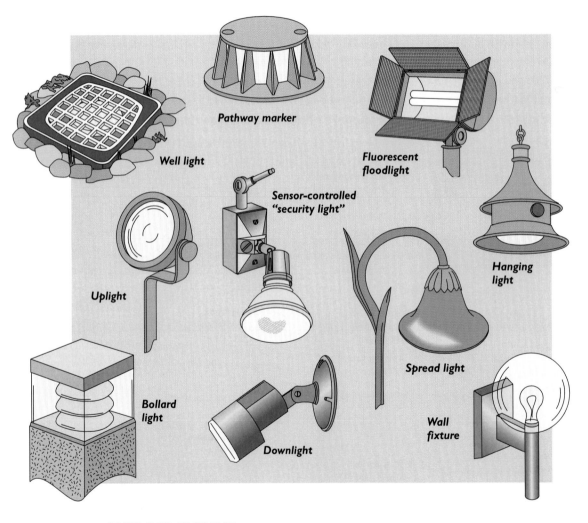

Pathway marker

Well light

Fluorescent floodlight

Sensor-controlled "security light"

Uplight

Hanging light

Bollard light

Spread light

Downlight

Wall fixture

OUTDOOR FIXTURES

Outdoor lighting fixtures come in many variations, some depicted above. Regardless of what you choose, you'll want to avoid glare. An opaque covering on a fixture will create a warm glow rather than a hot spot of light. You can also use lower light levels. At night, a little light goes a long way: 20 watts is considered "strong."

way that only the light playing on the tree branches, for example, not a bright spot, is noticed.

Lower light levels: At night, the view outside ends where the light ends. To create depth, divide the space into three zones: the foreground, which has a mid-level brightness; a softer middle ground; and a brighter background to direct the eye through the garden. Don't forget the view from inside the house. To avoid a black hole effect, strive to balance light levels on both sides of a window or sliding doors.

Downlighting
Use this technique to gently light up your porches, patios, and walkways. It's also good for accenting trees, shrubs, and flowers, while allowing you to see where you're going at night.

Diffused lighting
A low level of lighting is often enough for low-traffic areas. Light railings and fences indirectly from underneath or behind to outline the edges of the structures.

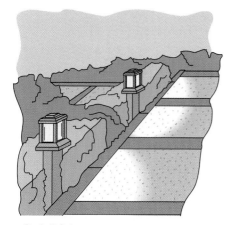

Path lighting
Low or slightly raised fixtures that spread soft pools of light can define a walkway and highlight elements of your garden.

OUTDOOR LIGHTING TECHNIQUES

You can use the fixtures shown on the previous page to light up your surroundings in various imaginative ways. Some standard lighting techniques are illustrated here. You can also combine techniques for interesting results. For example, a moonlight effect can be achieved by placing both uplights and downlights in a large tree. And don't forget, in food and cooking areas, you'll need stronger lights than you may want just for lounging.

Silhouetting
To silhouette a tree, shrub, or bed of flowers, try aiming a spotlight or wall washer at a fence or wall from close behind the plant.

Spread lighting
You can light up your shrubbery with spread lights in the planting beds themselves. Try different colored bulbs for different effects.

Creating a Patio Garden

Flowers can make any space come alive with color. A patio is a particularly good stage to show off beautiful plants. When placed against a simple paved background, pots of bright flowers create striking accents. Roses and vining plants can climb over many types of patio overheads. Patio plantings can also screen against wind and sun, disguise structural elements, and liven up drab corners or flat expanses of pavings. How you arrange different types of plants and flowers will help you define the character of the space. You can make a small area seem cozy or wide open, depending on the color and texture of the plants and where you site them.

As a general rule, choose flowers that have different bloom times and life cycles and envision how they will look from one season to the next. In addition to flowers, carefully selected foliage plants can provide a contrasting background to show off colorful blooms. The shapes and textures of the plants are equally important features to consider. Most avid gardeners will tell you that gardening is an art, with the garden as your canvas and the plants as the paints on your palette.

Ultimately, plant selection comes down to individual taste. However,

In a rustic brick-in-sand patio, generous plant pockets teem with flowers. The sundial and container plants add a touch of order to the pastoral setting.

Lath screening on a patio shelter opens to frame hanging plants, showing them off from both sides of the structure.

for general ideas on harmonizing colors, refer to the color wheel on page 41.

Container plants: Containers are a convenient and attractive means of introducing plants and flowers to a patio environment. Annuals, perennials, shrubs, and even vegetables can be moved about like pieces in a puzzle until the desired effect is achieved (trays with casters placed underneath the containers make moving them easy). You can even give your patio a new look several times a year by changing container plants to display the best each season. To get shade where there is none, set up a tree in a half barrel or tub. Containers also allow tender plants to winter over in a sheltered spot or on a sunny porch.

Hanging pots and baskets: When ground space is limited, plants can hang overhead or on walls. Hanging pots and baskets not only provide interesting texture and colorful accents, but also serve as shade and shelter, if thick enough. Moss-lined hanging baskets can be especially pretty. You can make them yourself by lining a metal frame with moist sphagnum moss, making holes in the side of the basket with your fingers, and inserting annuals in the holes. They're available at most nurseries, along with a variety of hanging baskets.

If you don't have an overhead structure, or if the headroom isn't enough for hanging plants, consider mounting baskets and built-in containers on a house wall; or install a lattice wall or metal screen and grow a "wall" of plants on it.

Plant pockets and crazy paving: There's no rule saying that patio plants must be confined to containers. It's a simple matter when planning your patio to leave out a few units of paving or to block off an open area when placing concrete. When construction is completed, plants can be fitted into the empty spaces.

Another traditional idea that creates a cottage garden feel is crazy paving—interspersing mosses, ground covers, or other low-lying plants among masonry units. You can even drill concrete paving so that drip tubing can be routed through to feed crevice plantings a small, steady diet.

Raised beds: Raised beds are great for making the most of a small area, or when you are searching for a simple way to add a design element to your garden.

Building a sturdy raised bed isn't very difficult, but if you plan to go higher than 3 feet or build on sloping or unstable soil, consult your local building code first.

Raised beds are box type or of the low, stepped-bed variety. You can vary the materials to get the form you want. Box-type beds range from 3 to 10 feet long, and from less than 1 foot to 3 feet high. They can be made of almost any

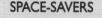

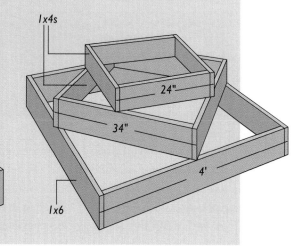

SPACE-SAVERS

An efficient way to use wooden box beds is to stack them "ziggurat-style." This type of raised bed can hold more than 20 different kinds of flowers and fits into a 4-by-4-foot space. A trellis adds a vertical element and extra growing space.

material you use for a wall, such as brick, concrete, stone, or wood—decay-resistant redwood, cedar, cypress, or pressure-treated lumber at least 2 inches thick.

Raised beds can harmonize with an existing garden design. You can work around irregular or difficult slopes in the lawn, for example, with a series of beds, providing a neat transition from one level to the next. By adding a wide top cap, a raised bed can provide extra room for potted plants or a comfortable place for a gardener to sit while weeding.

For a more finished look, you can stain plank boxes and then add detailing to tie the beds into the overall landscape design. To adapt the beds for a more rustic landscape, build the boxes out of railroad ties or logs—whole or cut in half.

A quick and effective way to soften the look of an expanse of uninterrupted paving is to introduce container plants. Dedicated gardeners sometimes rotate containers over the year to show off a succession of flowering plants.

With so many container styles to choose from, it's easy to find unusual examples that bring a unique element to your patio. This design has small, cupped openings on the side, allowing a variety of plants to grow in a single container.

Container plants, statue, and garden bench line the edge of a patio, defining the boundary between open, cultivated space and the garden of wildflowers beyond.

Looking After Your Flowers

To ensure that your time in the garden is well spent and that your plants flower brightly, proper plant care is essential.

Improving the soil: Soil doesn't always contain enough of the nutrients necessary for plant growth, so use fertilizers to make up for any shortfalls. These are most needed between the first growth of the year and the flowering period, usually from late winter to mid-spring.

Choose a lightweight, sterile potting soil designed for container gardening, never ordinary garden soil. You can buy potting soil at nurseries, garden centers, or from companies that sell topsoil. Plants in containers lose most of their nitrogen when water runs through the soil. Potting soils contain very few nutrients, so it's best to add liquid fertilizer right after planting and every two weeks after that.

As with containers, it's a good idea to use a good potting soil in raised bed gardening.

For raised beds with open bottoms, replace the soil below the boxes with amended soil that will improve the growing conditions. If the box has a solid bottom, drill holes. Before planting, soak the soil so it settles to a natural level.

Watering: For best plant performance, the soil should be moistened deeply. Roots are reticent about extending into dry soil; deeper watering will encourage deeper rooting, which protects plants from damage if surface moisture fluctuates.

Watering schedules for different types of plantings will vary with the climate, but as a rule, if you stick a finger into the soil and it feels dry, it's time to water. Container soil dries out quickly, so you might have to water more than once a day in

Herbs and flowers create a leafy green border between an adobe patio and stone retaining wall, softening the transition from paving to elevated garden.

very hot or windy weather. If the container feels light, or if the top 2 inches of the soil are dry, it's time to water. You know you've watered enough when water drips out the holes in the bottom of the container. If water runs down between the edges of the container and the earth, your root ball is probably too dry and has shrunk away from the pot edges. To fix this, partially submerge the container in a tub so the moisture can be absorbed by the roots.

To stretch the intervals between watering, mix super-absorbent soil polymers into your soil. These are available at most nurseries.

The easiest way to water a large number of containers or hanging plants is to run drip tubing and spray emitters to the pots. Check out your local nursery or irrigation supply store for suggestions.

Weeding: Keep weeds pulled or hoed from the very beginning. They rob desirable plants of water and nutrients while making your flower bed look unkempt.

Staking: If a plant starts to fall over or becomes too leggy when in bloom, it needs to be staked. Staking is usually necessary only with the tallest plants, or ones that are not getting enough sun. Different types of stakes and cylinders are available at nurseries or garden centers. The important thing is to support the flowers while concealing the stakes.

Separating the bulbs: If you have planted bulbs, note that their roots grow outward, new bulbs form, and sprout bulbs of their own, leading to crowding. With limited room for growth, the roots eventually begin to grow downward, into less fertile soil. When this occurs, usually after the first two years, bulbs will stop growing and flowering.

To get the most out of each bulb, pull up the plants during the dormant season and remove bulblets. Replant the smaller, newer bulbs in different areas.

Additional care: To keep your plants looking neat, cut back the stems, and prune and deadhead flowers, as in the illustration below. This will keep the garden tidy, and may encourage prolonged flowering and fruiting.

PROPER PRUNING

To maintain your plants, pinch off tips of new growth to induce branching lower on the stem (above). Cut spent flowers to curtail seed production, and to divert energy to the production of more flowers (right).

With palm trees arching overhead, and lush surrounding plantings, this patio resembles a shaded jungle clearing. Vegetation growing between the flagstone paving contributes to the effect.

Garden Planter/Bench

This garden bench—with the garden built right in—is designed to look good in virtually any patio setting. With the simple instructions featured on these two pages, you can build your own and sit in the shade of small planter trees or relax amid the beauty of your favorite plants.

BUYING THE RIGHT LUMBER

Use weatherproof clear redwood or cedar lumber. The list on the opposite page tells you how much wood to buy and how to cut it; the illustrations below show the assembly.

GETTING STARTED

To make each container base, butt two front and back pieces (B) between two side pieces (A) and nail them in place with 3¼-inch finishing nails. Nail a plywood bottom (I) to the base, using 2¾-inch nails Then drill five ¾-inch drain holes through the bottom piece.

Mark each side piece (E) end with the locations of the ¼-inch rods and ¼-inch lag screws (see Diagram 2). Next, counterbore ¾-inch-wide, 5⁄16-inch-deep holes for the washers, nuts, and bolt heads. Continue drilling ¼-inch holes for the bolts and rods.

Lay four D and four E pieces flat. Measure 2 inches from the lower edge and mark a line along the length of each board at that measurement. Build each container as shown in Diagram 1, aligning the top edge of the base with the marked lines on each of the two D and two E pieces. Nail a support (C), with the mitered edge up, into each container, using 2¾-inch nails.

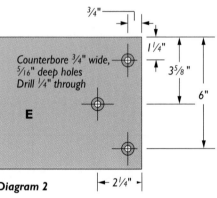

Counterbore ¾" wide, 5⁄16" deep holes
Drill ¼" through

E

¾"

1¼"

3⅝"

6"

2¼"

Diagram 2

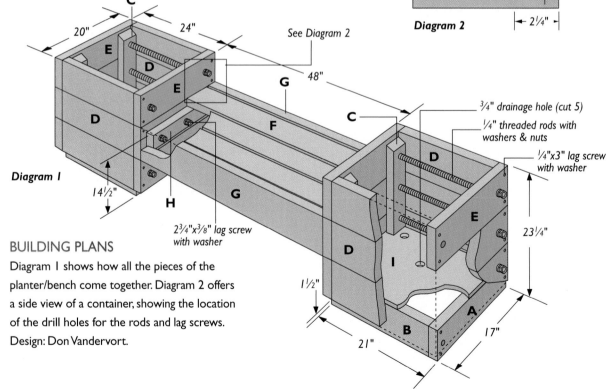

Diagram 1

C

20"

24"

E

D

E

See Diagram 2

48"

G

C

F

D

G

14½"

H

2¾"x³⁄8" lag screw with washer

I

¾" drainage hole (cut 5)

¼" threaded rods with washers & nuts

¼"x3" lag screw with washer

D

E

23¼"

D

1½"

B

21"

A

17"

BUILDING PLANS

Diagram 1 shows how all the pieces of the planter/bench come together. Diagram 2 offers a side view of a container, showing the location of the drill holes for the rods and lag screws. Design: Don Vandervort.

FINISHING THE CONTAINERS

Clamp four E pieces to the container supports (C). Use the ¼-inch holes in all the E pieces as guides to drill through the supports. Position four D pieces between sides (E). Clamp them in place by inserting rods, adding washers, and tightening nuts. Then secure each D piece by inserting ¼-inch lag screws through the remaining holes in the E pieces. Nail supports (C) to the upper four side pieces (E) with 2¾-inch nails. Drill three ⅜-inch holes in each bench support H and then bolt it to the containers with ⅜-inch lag screws and washers. Place containers in position before attaching the bench.

Set bench slats (F) on supports (H), spacing each slat evenly; nail in position with 3¼-inch finishing nails. Place bench faces (G) against front and back slat edges, keeping top edges flush; nail in place with 3¼-inch nails.

Set all visible nail heads, fill holes with wood putty, and sand exposed surfaces. Finish with water-repellent preservative.

	CUTTING LIST	
A	Container base sides	Four 2x4s @ 17"
B	Container base fronts and backs	Four 2x4s @ 18"
C	Container supports	Eight 2x4s @ 18"
D	Container fronts and backs	Twelve 2x8s @ 21"
E	Container sides	Twelve 2x8s @ 20"
F	Bench slats	Three 2x6s @ 48"
G	Bench faces	Two 2x8s @ 48"
H	Bench supports	Two 2x6s @ 17"
I	Container bottoms	Two pieces ¾" plywood @ 17"x21"
Galvanized threaded rods with washers and nuts		12 @ ¼"x2"
Galvanized lag screws		48 @ ¼"x3"
Galvanized lag screws with washers		6 @ ⅜"x2¾"
Galvanized finishing nails		3¼"
Galvanized finishing nails		2¾"
Wood putty		
Water-repellent wood preservative		

BASIC BENCHES

If instead of a planter/bench you would rather build a regular bench, follow these simple steps. For a straight bench, saw shoulders in 4-by-4 posts (A) and set in place; then bolt 2-by-4 braces (B) to the posts and nail on the planks (C). For a corner bench, mark posts (D), saw shoulders and add braces (E), and then nail on the mitered planks (F).

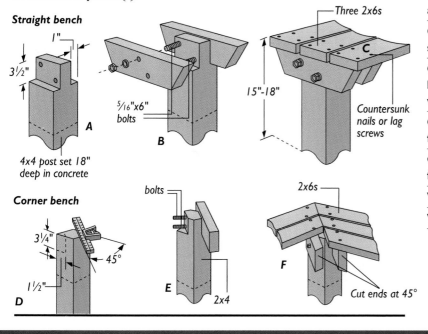

Straight bench

1"

3½"

4x4 post set 18" deep in concrete

A

⁵⁄₁₆"x6" bolts

B

15"-18"

Three 2x6s

C

Countersunk nails or lag screws

Corner bench

3¼"

1½"

D

45°

bolts

E

2x4

2x6s

F

Cut ends at 45°

Building
TECHNIQUES

This chapter sets out the procedures you'll need to follow if you plan to build a patio on your own. It begins with information on buying materials and safety gear, before moving on to describe how to prepare the site and lay edgings—two prerequisites to a successful patio project. Construction methods, which vary from one patio material to the next, are also addressed in this chapter. You'll find tips on working with brick, concrete, pavers, ceramic tiles, adobe, stone, wood, and loose materials. In addition, the construction of such complementary structural elements as retaining walls, drainage systems, and steps is explained. As with any building project, always check with your building department about code restrictions that may apply to your project. Also, be sure to to take into account soil, drainage, and frost conditions in your area. Local officials and landscape professionals can be a real help here.

Interlocking concrete pavers fit like puzzle pieces on a bed of sand. They are tapped into place quickly with a mallet and provide an attractive, long-lasting surface.

Getting Started

Before finalizing plans for your patio, drop by your local building department and inquire about regulations that may apply to your project. Building officials can be of great assistance in pointing you in the right direction. Their job is to enforce the building code, which is a set of regulations that specifies minimum standards for materials and workmanship. Constructing your patio—or any project—to these standards is cheap insurance; following the code will help assure you of the structural integrity of whatever you build.

TOOLS OF THE TRADE

You may have to invest in some of the specialized tools shown in this section: when working with concrete, for example, the magnesium hand float, jointer, and edger are all important. Some tools can be improvised. The bladed strikeoff must be built to the specifications of the job. The darby (*below*) can also be homemade; while the extra-long mason's level (*right*) can be replaced with an ordinary level laid against a straight 2-by-4.

To place masonry units, you will also need a number of tools that you likely already have: shovels, a wheelbarrow, a small sledgehammer, a rubber mallet, and a carpenter's square.

CONCRETE MASONRY TOOLS

Bull float
Smooths the surface of very large concrete projects. Homemade from 1-by lumber and a swiveling attachment, such as used for wall-sander. Insert threaded end of broom handle into attachment.

Plumb bob
Used to transfer verticals, such as from guide strings, to form boards.

Kneeboard
For kneeling on plastic concrete when smoothing surface. Homemade using 2x2s and 1/2" plywood.

Strikeoff
Levels a sand or mortar base. Also for leveling cast concrete. The bladed strikeoff shown here is built for the job, using 2-by lumber for the handle and 1-by for the blade. For some jobs, use a straight piece of wood only.

Darby
Smooths the surface of large concrete projects.

Edger
For smoothing and compacting the edges of concrete.

Dash brush
For dashing mortar or color onto concrete. A wallpaper brush can be used instead.

Jointer
Creates control joints in concrete.

Tamper
For compacting gravel fill. Homemade using 2x4 lumber and 3/4" plywood. Steel tamper can be rented.

Magnesium hand float
Gives a smooth finish to outdoor concrete.

Square shovel
Use when working with concrete.

Mortar hoe
For mixing mortar and concrete by hand.

Convex jointer
For striking mortar joints. Piece of 1/2" or 3/4" copper tube bent to shape can be substituted.

Wood float
For smoothing the surface of concrete.

UNIT MASONRY TOOLS

Stone chisel
For scoring and cutting
stones. A brickset can
be used instead.

Brickset
For scoring and
cutting bricks.

Mortar box
Handy for mixing
mortar. A large plastic
tub can also be used.

Rubber mallet
Used to tap paving
units into place.

Tape measure
Extra-long model (50')
is best. Keep handy for
laying out projects.

Hand-drilling hammer
Used to tap brickset or
stone chisel.

Joint-striking tools
For striking mortar joints. Convex
jointer (top right); a piece of 1/2"
to 3/4" copper tube bent to shape
can be substituted. V-jointer
(lower right).

Tile cutter
Cuts tile to the
required size.

Chalk line
For laying out
long, straight
reference lines
on masonry
surface.

Mason's level
An extra-long wooden
level for checking both level and
plumb; long wooden carpenter's level
can also be used.

Joint filler
Pushes mortar
into long joints.

**Pointing
trowel**
For tooling
weathered,
struck, and
flush mortar
joints.

Tile nipper
Removes small
pieces of tile.

Rubber-backed trowel
Used to apply grout.

Mason's trowel
Used to spread mortar
on masonry units.

**Mason's line
and blocks**
Marks height
of each course
of masonry.

Sled jointer
For tooling joints
in block walls.

Notched trowel
Essential for applying adhesive.
Ask your tile dealer for the correct
size of notches for your project.

Mortar hoe
For mixing
mortar and
concrete by
hand.

**Bricklayer's
hammer**
One end for tapping
bricks into place in
mortar; pointed end
for scraping away
mortar and scoring
and cutting bricks.

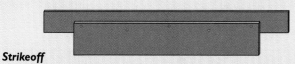

Strikeoff
Levels a sand or mortar base for paving. Also used for cast concrete. Built
to required depth for each job; use straight 2-by lumber for the handle and
1-by for the blade. For some jobs, use straight piece of wood only.

Shopping Around

Standard patio paving materials represent the full range of masonry products—brick, stone, tile, pavers, and concrete. Each offers a combination of beauty, utility, ease of maintenance, and all are highly resistant to natural deterioration. However, depending on the specific paving material you choose, there are certain factors to keep in mind when shopping around.

Brick: You can find most types of brick at masonry suppliers or building and landscape supply yards; look in the Yellow Pages under "Brick" or "Building Materials." For secondhand brick and used companion materials, such as cobblestones and wood timbers, salvage yards are often good sources.

When you order, ask about delivery charges. Though they're usually low, they're often not included in the quoted price. Paying a little more to have the bricks delivered on a pallet prevents the considerable breakage that can result when the bricks are merely dumped off a truck.

Make sure your dealer has enough of the bricks you need to complete your project. If you have to use a different variety or some bricks from another supplier, you may not be able to complete the pattern you've started.

Ceramic tile: Installing ceramic tile can be a sizable financial commitment. Choosing a tile that meets both functional and decorative needs requires careful thought. Take time to shop around, calculate cost, and order carefully.

Ceramic tile manufacturers, distributors, and dealers, as well as some licensed contractors, have showrooms displaying a great variety of tile. However, keep in mind that most retailers have displays (or catalogs) of tiles they don't have in stock; you may have to wait a long time for certain tiles, so plan accordingly. Before you bring the tile home, check the cartons to be

BASIC SAFETY GEAR

Many tasks involved in building a patio require the basic safety gear shown here. For example, dry portland cement is irritating to the eyes, nose, and mouth; wear goggles and a dust mask when working with it. As well, cutting stone or masonry units causes chips to fly; wear goggles to protect eyes.

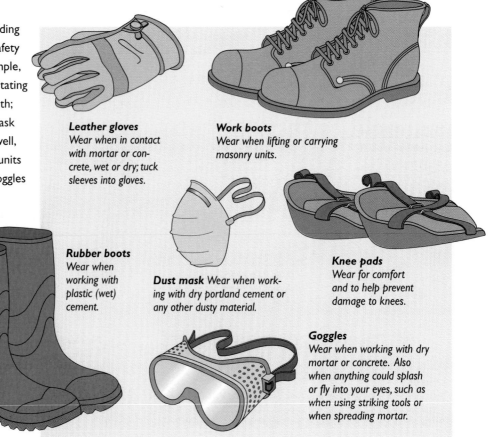

Leather gloves
Wear when in contact with mortar or concrete, wet or dry; tuck sleeves into gloves.

Work boots
Wear when lifting or carrying masonry units.

Rubber boots
Wear when working with plastic (wet) cement.

Dust mask Wear when working with dry portland cement or any other dusty material.

Knee pads
Wear for comfort and to help prevent damage to knees.

Goggles
Wear when working with dry mortar or concrete. Also when anything could splash or fly into your eyes, such as when using striking tools or when spreading mortar.

sure the shades of color in the tiles match. Different cartons of the same tile can differ significantly.

There are several ways to save on tiles. One is to watch for close-outs. A dealer will often sell close-outs at a discount. These may be tiles that the manufacturer has discontinued, a color or pattern that was overstocked, or a supply of tiles left over from a large installation or a canceled order.

Another way to save money when buying tile is to purchase "seconds." These tiles are flawed or blemished (usually only slightly), so they cannot be sold with the regular stock at full price. Often seconds will go undetected if randomly mixed with unblemished tile.

Concrete pavers: Concrete pavers are available at most building and garden supply centers. In general, size and texture will determine the cost of the units. A seeded paver can cost up to three times more than a plain or colored one of the same size, for example.

Stone: Stoneyards supply uncut (rubble) or cut (ashlar) stone. Cut stones are more expensive.

Flagstone paving used to be more common than it is today, but still provides one of the toughest outdoor surfaces available. The subdued colors and irregular shapes greatly enhance most outdoor settings. River rock and fieldstone offer alternatives to the high cost of flagstone.

Adobe: If you live close to a source, adobe can be less expensive per square foot than brick. However, if you live outside the Southwest, delivery charges may add considerably to the cost.

Most adobe is sold through dealers (check the Yellow Pages under the heading "Building Materials"). Always buy at least a dozen extra adobe blocks—a few are likely to come with irregularities or will develop flaws once you put them down.

BUYING CONCRETE

Depending on how much time and money you're willing to invest, you can make up your own concrete mix from scratch, buy a pre-packaged mix, haul your own plastic (wet) mix, or have ready-mix delivered by truck.

Bulk dry materials: You usually save money by ordering your materials and doing your own mixing. For small projects, though, surcharges for small-quantity delivery can eat up your savings, so check carefully before ordering, and explore the alternatives. The most economical option is to haul the materials yourself.

Dry pre-packaged mix: Bagged, dry concrete mix is hard to beat for convenience. Though it is a very expensive way of buying concrete, it can be the most economical on small jobs; simply add water and mix yourself.

Haul-it-yourself plastic mix: Some dealers supply trailers containing concrete with the water already added. These carry about one cubic yard of concrete; you haul it yourself with your car. At best, the trailer may have a revolving drum to mix the concrete as you go, or it may be a simple metal or fiberglass box into which the concrete is placed. A word of caution: These trailers are very heavy; be sure your tires and brakes are in good shape and your vehicle and trailer hitch are rated for the weight.

Ready-mix: A commercial ready-mix truck is the best choice for large-scale work. The truck can deliver a big quantity all at once, so you can finish large projects in a single placement. Look up concrete plants in the Yellow Pages; keep in mind that many have minimum orders, so be sure to check.

A concrete pumping contractor can supply special equipment to reach awkward spots. The pump forces ready-mixed concrete through a long hose that can be run over fences and around houses.

Preparing the Site

Regardless of the material you choose for your patio, you will have to excavate the site and prepare a foundation or sub-base. This is probably the most important stage in the entire project. The foundation affects the patio's life span and its finished appearance. Since the base you lay will depend on your paving material, be sure to consult the section on that particular material for specific requirements.

Most properties just need minor leveling; some may also require a short retaining wall *(page 137)*. However the grading of some sites—low-lying areas, steep slopes,

and areas with unstable soil, for example—can pose serious problems. In these cases, it's best to consult a landscape architect or landscape contractor. Be on the lookout for underground water, gas, or electrical lines. These systems, plus lawn sprinklers or existing drains, may need rerouting before you proceed.

GRADING

For most patio projects, grading will involve digging out the area to be paved, making sure to provide proper drainage *(page 135)*. Try to avoid filling and tamping; tamped

earth is never as firm as undisturbed soil, and will inevitably settle, taking your paving with it.

The first step to preparing the site is laying out the area to be paved with mason's lines and batterboards, as shown on the facing page. When building a square or rectangular patio, ensure the corners form perfect right angles. As you lay out the corners of the patio area, measure a triangle *(opposite)* with sides 3 feet, 4 feet, and 5 feet long, or multiples of those dimensions such as 6-8-10, 9-12-15, or 12-16-20 feet. For maximum accuracy, use the largest multiple possible.

GRADING OVERVIEW

This illustration shows how a perfectly graded site improves overall drainage. The land slopes away from structures so the runoff is directed toward the street or a swale (low-lying stretch of land).

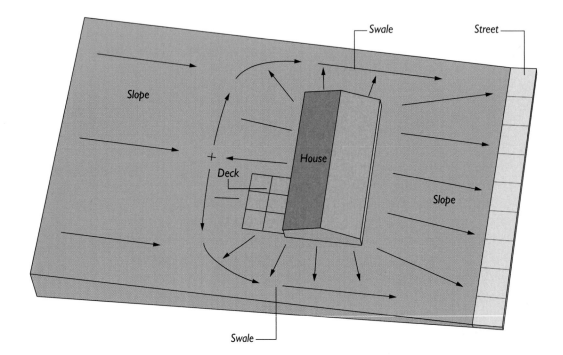

When laying a patio next to a house or any other structure, plan to leave a gap of at least 1/2-inch or more where the patio surface meets the building. Galvanized metal flashing protects wood siding or floor framing from damage due to moisture.

The patio's perimeter lines are transferred to stakes *(see page 134)*. This way, line height can be adjusted to reflect the standard pitch a patio requires for drainage.

Before grading begins, additional stakes and mason's lines are installed to create a gridwork that acts as a guide in excavation.

Irregular patio shapes call for additional stakes and lines—the 3-4-5 triangle method can still be used to ensure any corners are at perfect right angles.

In contrast, arcs or circles are relatively simple to lay out. Just determine the radius of the curve with a string compass—essentially a string nailed to the ground at one end and to a stake at the other *(page 141)*. The stake traces and marks the desired curve.

Laying out the patio

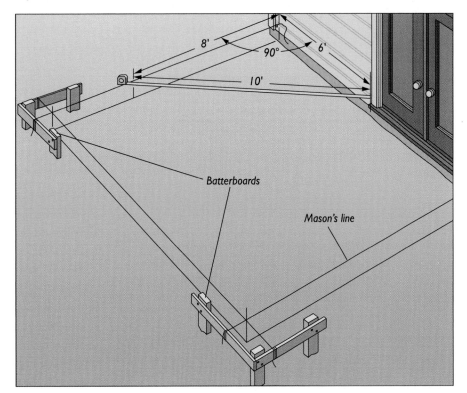

Batterboards

Mason's line

Setting up perimeter lines

After determining the preferred level of the finished surface, hammer a nail into the house where the corner of the patio will meet it. Set up batterboards about 18 inches beyond the corresponding outside corner of the patio. Stretch a length of mason's line from the nail to the batterboards. To square the corner, measure 6 feet along the wall and mark this point. Then put a mark on the string with a piece of tape 8 feet away from the wall. Move the string back and forth along the batterboard until the diagonal is exactly 10 feet. Hammer a nail into the batterboard at this spot and attach the string to it. Repeat this procedure at the other end of the patio. Finally, measure the same distance down both of the side lines, mark each line, and attach a third line parallel to the house, marking the outside edge of the patio.

Grading for a patio

1 Measuring the grade
Using the batterboards and mason's lines as guides, drive stakes into the ground at the corners of the patio next to the house, and at the outside corners. Mark the desired patio level on the stakes next to the house. Attach a line at the mark and stretch it toward the outside corner stake; level the string with a line level *(inset)*. Mark the outside corner stake where the line crosses it. Repeat for the other stakes. Calculate the distance you need to drop the strings to achieve a standard grade of 1 inch every 8 feet (sloping away from the house) and mark it on each outside stake below the level mark. Working from your perimeter lines, add more lines and stakes to form a grid for reference while excavating *(above, right)*.

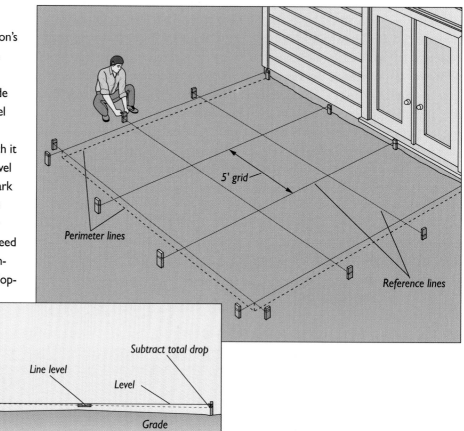

5' grid

Perimeter lines

Reference lines

Subtract total drop

Line level

Level

Grade

2 Excavating the site
Measure down from the lines, and excavate a distance equal to the combined thickness of the paving and the setting bed, keeping in mind the required slope for drainage. Take shallow scoops with a square-sided shovel to remove the minimum soil required, leaving the soil below undisturbed. To even out low spots, spread sand evenly with a rake, moisten it, then tamp several times with a hand tamper or a rented power vibrator.

Whenever you pave an area, its drainage is affected, since water tends to run off even the most porous paving.

Unless the area to be paved slopes naturally, it must be graded before paving so that runoff won't collect where it will cause problems—against a house foundation, for example. A paved surface should slope at least one inch every eight feet (or $1/8$ inch per foot).

Often, the bed below the paving, whether it's sand or a thicker layer of gravel, will provide adequate drainage. But sometimes, additional provisions are necessary. Shown here are three different drainage systems that effectively handle runoff around a paved site. If your backyard needs one of these systems, and you plan to do the work yourself, remember that both the surface drain box and perforated drainpipe setup require placing concrete. For tips on working with concrete, turn to page 164.

DRAINAGE SYSTEMS

Shown below are three common drainage systems that can be installed under paved surfaces.

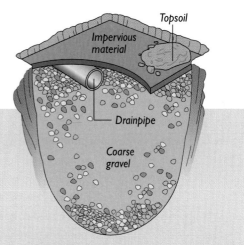

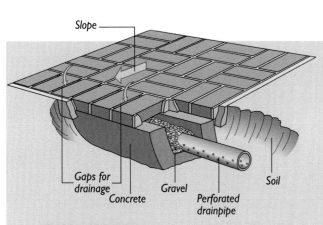

Perforated drainpipe
Perforated drainpipes drain water from under pavings. Place pipe, perforated side down, in a trench dug 12 inches deep (deeper in frost areas) under the center or around the edge of the site. Pack in 6 inches of gravel and replace with soil. To route a drainage trench through a mortared patio, as shown, first form a concrete channel; then leave open (ungrouted) joints between units bridging the trench.

Dry well
To build a dry well, dig a 2- to 4-foot-wide hole at least 3 feet deep (keep the bottom above the water table). Cover the sides of the hole with geotextile fabric. Next, dig trenches for the drain pipes that will carry water into the dry well. Fill the dry well with coarse gravel or small rocks, then cover it with impervious material, such as heavy roofing felt, and conceal it with topsoil.

Catch basin
To drain water from a low-lying area, install a catch basin, digging the hole for it at the lowest point. Set a ready-made concrete box (available at building supply stores) into the hole or place the concrete yourself. Set a grate on top and dig a sloping trench from the hole for a drainpipe to direct water toward a dry well or storm drain (if permitted).

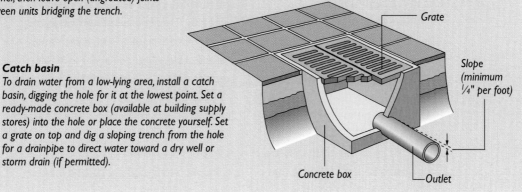

Demolishing an Existing Patio

To remove an old concrete or asphalt surface, you'll need a lot of elbow grease as well as the right hand tools—a sledgehammer, crowbar and pike—or a jackhammer. You can rent the tools you don't have; just be sure that each tool has been checked for safety.

Wearing shatterproof goggles or safety glasses is an absolute must when you work with tools that send chips of hard material flying. It's also wise to wear heavy leather gloves, long pants, sturdy shoes, and hearing protectors or ear plugs.

Sledgehammers and crowbars: Wielded by strong arms, a sledgehammer or a 4- or 5-foot crowbar works surprisingly quickly, depending on the thickness of the paving to be removed. A large pike will perform extremely well on 3-inch-thick asphalt on a cool day. A small jackhammer should be just as fast. On hot days, however, asphalt takes on the consistency of tar, comes loose in tiny chunks, and sticks to clothes and tools.

Jackhammers: Pneumatic jackhammers, the heavyweights of concrete demolition, operate by air supplied by a compressor, which in turn is run by a gasoline or diesel engine. The compressed air is delivered to the jackhammer through a heavy-duty hose.

Jackhammer units are usually rented on a trailer that you tow behind your car. Many rental outfits offer a choice of sizes—jackhammers that operate with 30, 60, or 90 cubic feet of air per minute (cfm). Each jackhammer weighs about the same number of pounds as its cfm rating.

The lightest model, the 30-pounder, is best used for breaking up asphalt 2 to 3 inches thick. Sixty-pound jackhammers handle concrete up to 4 inches thick—the depth of most patios and driveways. Ninety-pound jackhammers can break through concrete up to 12 inches thick (foundations for example), but they wear you out in the process.

Electric jackhammers are smaller, lighter in weight, and quieter than pneumatic ones. They're also less powerful, running on 120-volt household current. Use them on small areas of relatively thin (3 inches or less) concrete or asphalt. Never use electric jackhammers under damp or wet conditions.

The removable tip of a jackhammer is called a point or tool. The type of point required varies with the job to be done. Take care when changing or removing steel points: Points that become heated by friction can burn an ungloved hand.

When you're operating a jackhammer, let the machine do the work. If you lean on the tool, you'll be in for a bone jarring ride. Use your hands and arms only to balance the tool. It's easiest to break off the concrete in manageable 3- to 5-inch chunks.

If the point gets embedded with no sign of the concrete cracking, pull it out immediately and move closer to the edge. Otherwise you'll risk embedding the point so tightly that getting it out could be difficult.

If your house sits on a sloping lot, you may need a retaining wall in your patio plan. The safest way to build a retaining wall is to locate it at the bottom of a gentle slope and fill in behind it with soil.

Retaining walls must have adequate drainage to prevent water from building up behind them. Surface water can be collected in a shallow ditch along the top of the wall. Subsurface water can be collected in a gravel backfill and channeled away either through a drainpipe behind the wall or through weep holes spaced along the wall at ground level. (Weep holes may require a ditch along the base to prevent water from spilling onto the patio.)

Make sure all drainpipes and ditches are properly sloped to direct water to an appropriate disposal site.

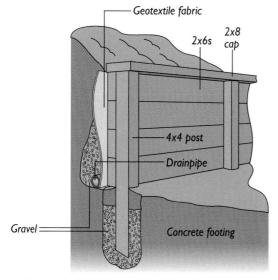

Dimension lumber

This type of wall can be made of decay-resistant dimension lumber (such as redwood heartwood or treated lumber) set vertically or horizontally. Moisture-proof building paper helps preserve the wood. Anchor the posts in concrete and use a 2-by-6 cap to strengthen the wall and provide a garden seat.

RETAINING WALLS IN PROFILE

Building a retaining wall can be demanding work. High walls especially have to be well built and sturdy, because of the enormous weight of the soil they hold back. Most localities require a building permit for all retaining walls; many require that a licensed engineer design and supervise the construction of walls over 3 feet.

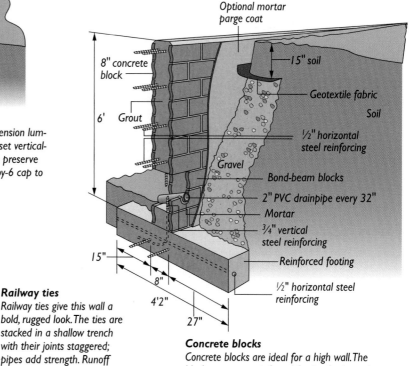

Concrete blocks

Concrete blocks are ideal for a high wall. The blocks rest on a reinforced footing; horizontal reinforcing can be added as needed. A ¾-inch coat of mortar, or parge coat, troweled onto the back of the wall will help to control dampness on the face. Consult your building department before attempting such a complex job.

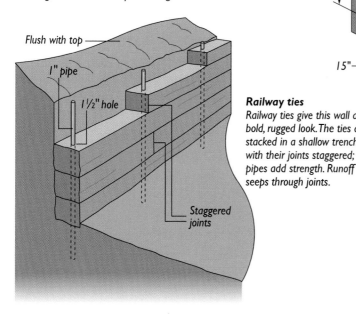

Railway ties

Railway ties give this wall a bold, rugged look. The ties are stacked in a shallow trench with their joints staggered; pipes add strength. Runoff seeps through joints.

Building Edgings

Almost any patio or walkway will require some type of edging. In addition to outlining the space, edgings confine the surface material within the desired area, an important function when working with loose materials, casting concrete, or laying brick or pavers in sand. When used to curb paved areas, edgings are usually installed after the base has been prepared, but before the paving is laid. Edgings are often made of wood, but other materials can also provide the same defining and containing functions with attractive results, as shown on the next few pages.

If you are planning to use a wood edging, choose a wood that is highly resistant to rot and termites, such as pressure-treated lumber or the heartwood of cedar, redwood, or certain types of cypress. Redwood is a good choice for benderboard (for curved edgings).

Brick-in-soil edgings are the easiest to make, but you must have firm soil to hold the bricks. "Invisible" concrete edgings are small, underground concrete footings that secure paving units without visible support. This strong edging design works well with brick-in-sand paving and is adapt-able to interlocking concrete pavers, regular paving blocks, and other units. Concrete edgings can also be built so they are even with the paved surface.

Manufactured plastic edgings are an easy-to-install option for do-it-yourselfers. The strips secure bricks or concrete pavers below finished paving height. They can be concealed by soil and sod. Flexible sections negotiate tight curves, rigid strips can also follow curves if kerfed—notched with a saw for the length of the curve. Plastic edgings are secured with oversize (10- to 12-inch) spikes.

Installing wood edgings

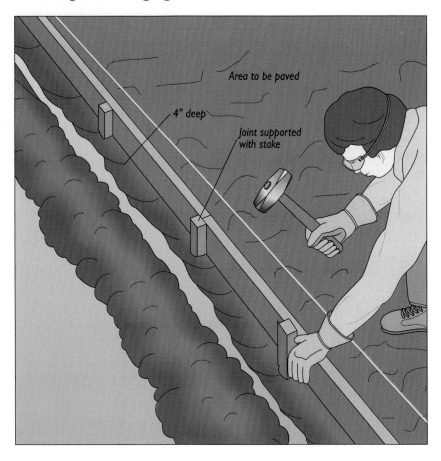

Area to be paved

4" deep

Joint supported with stake

1 Constructing the edging
Drive several 12-inch stakes (1x3s or 2x2s) into the soil, aligning their inner faces with the perimeter lines laid out prior to grading. Position the edging boards against the inside faces of the stakes, level with the lines, and fasten the stakes to the boards. Go back and place additional stakes no more than 4 feet apart. Where edging boards are butted, add doubled stakes or splice the boards. Join corner boards together with galvanized screws or box nails.

2 Filling in

Cut off the tops of the stakes at an angle, as shown; then pack excavated soil around the outside of the edgings (this will hide the stakes).

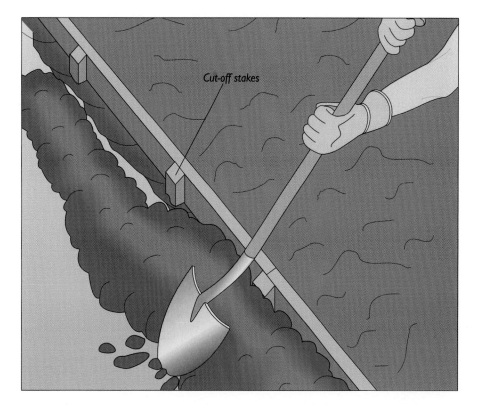

Cut-off stakes

Installing brick-in-soil edgings

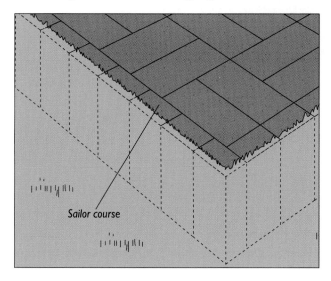

Sailor course

Tilted sailor course

Building two types of brick edging

Brick-in-soil edgings are easy to construct, but the earth must be really firm to hold the bricks securely. For the type of edging shown above left, cut a narrow trench deep enough to bury the full length of a brick (unless the area has already been graded deep enough). Install a row of "sailors"— bricks standing on end—leveling the tops as you go. Pack earth tightly against the outer perimeter of the bricks to secure them.

For the type of edging shown above right, install the sailor course tilted at 45°. This gives a notched effect at the edge and allows the pavement to rise above the grade, at the same time keeping as much of the brick edging underground as possible.

Installing an invisible edging

1 Casting the concrete

Place concrete *(page 164)* between temporary form boards made of 2x8 lumber, set one brick length apart, and nailed to 2x2 or 1x4 stakes. Use a strikeoff to level the concrete one brick thickness below the top of the form. (The concrete should be about 4" thick.) As you move the strikeoff along, place bricks in the plastic concrete. Tap them in place with a rubber mallet.

These edgings can be adapted to other types of units by adjusting the distance between the form boards and the depth of the concrete below the surface.

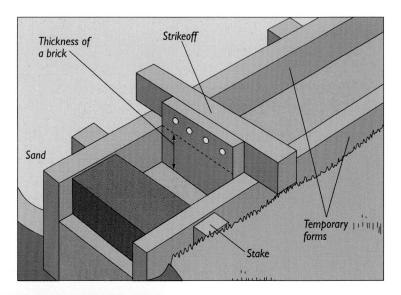

2 Leveling the sand

The next day, remove the forms. After the concrete has cured, use the completed edging as a guide to strike off the sand, and then begin the brick-in-sand paving.

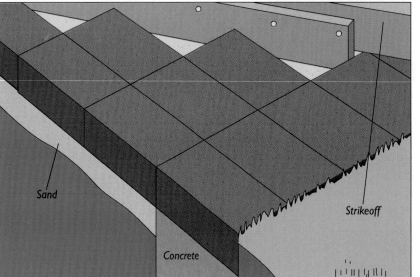

Installing concrete edgings

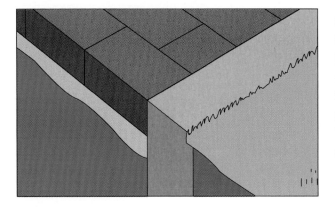

Striking the concrete

Concrete edgings are constructed in a manner similar to invisible edgings, except that the concrete is placed higher, to be level with the masonry units. Use 2x4 lumber for the temporary form. Level the concrete with a straight 2x4. Move it slowly along the form with a zigzag motion. Make two passes this way. You can finish the surface of the concrete in a variety of ways; see pages 172 to 175 for a few ideas.

Building a curved form

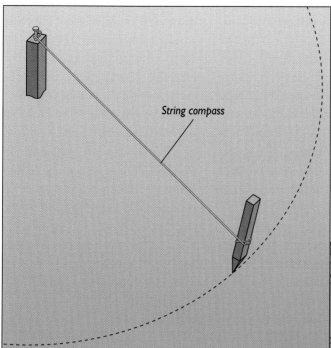

String compass

1 Determining the radius
Determine the radius with a compass made of two stakes and a length of string. Dig the pointed end of the outer stake into the ground to mark the curve.

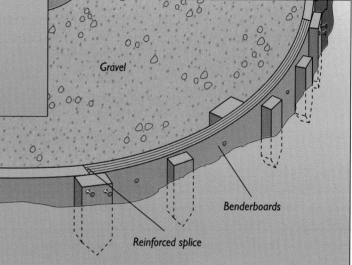

Gravel

Benderboards

Reinforced splice

2 Bending the form
Bend several layers of benderboard (thin, rot-resistant boards, usually redwood or cedar) against the stakes until you have a thickness equal to the other form boards. Drive in some nails or drywall screws to keep the layers together. Add an inside stake and pull it up as the concrete is placed.

Forming very tight curves

Very tight curves, such as the one illustrated at right, can be formed only with sheet metal, plastic, or other thin, flexible material. Cut the material to size and nail it to the stakes. Add extra stakes for additional support, if necessary.

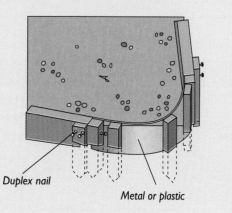

Duplex nail

Metal or plastic

Working with Mortar

Mortar is the "glue" that binds masonry units together and holds them to a concrete slab. In addition, it seals out wind and water, compensates for variations in the size of masonry units, and provides various decorative effects, depending on how the joints are tooled.

Ingredients: The recipes for masonry mortar vary according to their use, but the ingredients are always the same: portland cement, sand, masonry cement, and water. (Mortar for paving differs from other mortar recipes as it contains no lime. You can use cement-lime mortars for pavers, providing the lime or the cement is air-entrained.) Consult your building supplier about the quantity of mortar you'll need. Mortar sand should be clean, sharp-edged, and free of impurities such as salt, clay, dust, and organic matter. Never use beach sand—its grains are too rounded. Use drinkable water for mortar; never salt water or water high in acid or alkali content.

Measuring: The most accurate way to proportion ingredients is to weigh them, but because this is rarely practical, masons usually go by volume. Recipes for various types of mortar are given below. Once you're ready to begin, you'll probably find it more convenient to measure out ingredients by the bag, bucket or shovelful. The key is to be consistent in measuring so that your mortar will be the same from batch to batch. Since mortar must be mixed in fairly small batches, you may find it useful to mix it by the shovelful.

Mortar becomes weaker with increased sand content, but it also becomes cheaper, as the amount of cement—the most expensive ingredient—goes down in proportion. Type S mortar offers a good medium strength and workability for above and below ground use.

MIXING MORTAR

When mixing mortar, the dry ingredients are first measured out and then mixed, either in a power mixer or by hand, then the water is added and mixed in. The amount of water depends on the composition of the mortar and the absorption rate of the masonry units to be laid, factors that vary according to the weather. The mortar should have a smooth, buttery consistency; it should spread well and stick to vertical surfaces, yet not smear the work. Add water a little at a time until these requirement have been met.

Using a power mixer: For large jobs, power mixers can be rented in a variety of sizes. With the mixer running, add some water and half the sand. CAUTION: Never put the shovel inside the mixer.

Next, add all of the cement, the rest of the sand, and enough water to achieve the right consistency. The mixer should run for three or four minutes once all the water is added. Mix only enough to last about two hours; any more might stiffen before it is used.

Mixing by hand: Small amounts of mortar can readily be mixed by hand. You'll need a wheelbarrow or a mortar box, and a hoe. Thoroughly mix the sand and cement before adding the water. Hoe the combined dry ingredients into a pile, make a hole in the top, and add some water. Lastly, mix in the water and repeat as necessary to achieve a smooth, uniform, consistency.

MASONRY MORTAR FORMULAS (BY PARTS)				
TYPE	PORTLAND CEMENT	MASONRY CEMENT	MASONRY SAND	CHIEF CHARACTERISTIC
M	1	1	6	High compressive strength
N	–	1	3	More workable
S	1/2	1	4 1/2	Best blend of workability and strength

Building Brick Patios

Once you get the hang of it, brick-laying takes on a certain rhythm all its own, making for enjoyable, satisfying work. Even the tools and techniques you'll need are basic.

As discussed beginning on page 52, you have many options in brick types, textures, and colors. Patio patterns can be as creative as your imagination—and your brick-cutting skills—dictate. See below to learn how to cut a brick.

Brick paving methods include placing bricks in sand *(page 144)*, dry mortar *(page 145)*, and wet mortar *(page 146)*. The first technique is easiest for beginners; dry mortar is a variation of the brick-in-sand method. The wet mortar method produces the most formal results.

As with most masonry work, successful bricklaying depends on proper preparation of the base. The ground should be solid. If you have to lay bricks on fill, be sure that it has settled for a long time, preferably at least a year. The fill should always be dampened and tamped before you lay the bricks. A bit of dry cement powder will help hold fill in place.

You can also lay brick on an existing concrete slab that's clean and in good condition. To support paving of any kind, the slab must be reinforced with wire mesh. Check the slab for cracks; if they are not more than $\frac{1}{16}$ inch wide, the slab is probably reinforced. If the cracks are wider than $\frac{1}{16}$ inch the slab may still function as a base, but you should consult a pro for installation tips.

Cutting Brick

No matter how carefully you plan, some brick cutting is almost inevitable. Save your cutting for last so you can do it all at once when you're certain of the exact sizes and shapes you need.

If you have just a few cuts to make, the best tool is the brickset.

Tap the brick lightly to score a groove across all four sides before the final blow. Set the brick on flat sand and place the brickset (with the bevel facing away from the piece to be used) along the cut line. Tap the brickset sharply with a small sledgehammer. If necessary, chip away the rough edges with the brickset or a mason's hammer.

If you have a lot of cutting to do, you can rent a hydraulic brick cutter. For repeated angle cuts, a diamond-bladed tub saw is the best bet *(page 148)*.

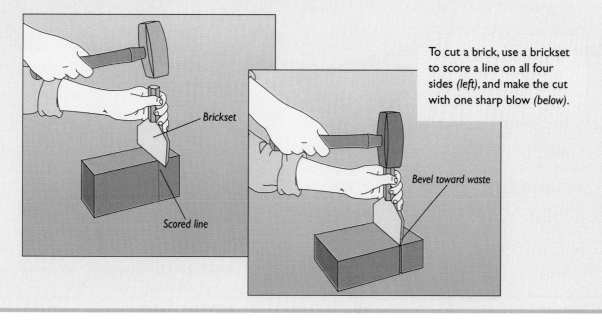

Brickset

Scored line

To cut a brick, use a brickset to score a line on all four sides *(left)*, and make the cut with one sharp blow *(below)*.

Bevel toward waste

Laying bricks in sand

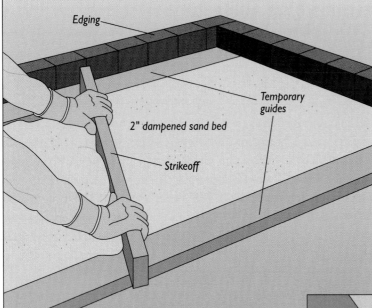

Edging

Temporary guides

2" dampened sand bed

Strikeoff

1 Striking off the base

After grading the area to be paved and constructing edgings, you can begin to lay the sand base. Set temporary guides inside the edgings, their top surfaces one brick-thickness below the finished grade. If you use 2x4s, as shown, the sand bed will be approximately 2" deep. Place dampened sand between the guides; strike it off smooth, about 3' at a time, with a straight piece of lumber.

Tamp the sand, then restrike if necessary. If your project is narrow enough, you can also use the bladed strikeoff, resting on the edgings, instead of using the temporary guides.

2 Setting the bricks or pavers

Working from a corner outward, place the bricks, tapping them into place with a mallet or piece of wood. A mason's string aids alignment. Remove the temporary guides as you work, and use a trowel to fill in the area with sand. Strike off the area where the guide was with a short board. Use the leveled section as a guide, being careful not to disturb it.

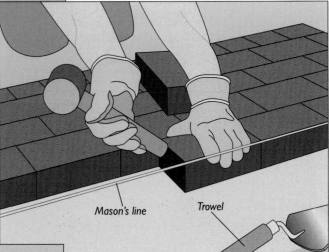

Mason's line

Trowel

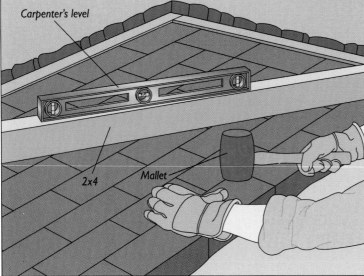

Carpenter's level

2x4

Mallet

3 Checking level as you go

Check level often as you lay bricks. When necessary, tap bricks down with a mallet. A straight 2x4 helps a carpenter's level bridge a larger area. Use a steel trowel to smooth sand while you work.

4 Sanding the joints
Spread fine sand over the surface of the finished paving. Let it dry thoroughly, then sweep it into the joints. Add sand until joints are full. Use a fine spray to wet the finished paving down; this will help settle the sand.

Bench brush

Laying bricks in dry mortar

1 Placing bricks and mortar
After following step 1 on the previous page, set bricks with ½" open joints (use a ½" thick wooden spacer and a mason's string for alignment). Mix dry cement and sand in a 1:4 ratio, and spread it over the surface, brushing it into the open joints. Kneel on a board to avoid disturbing the paving. Then, carefully sweep the excess mortar off the bricks.

Scrub brush

Mortar

Wooden tamper

2 Tamping the mortar
Use a piece of ½" thick wood to tamp the dry mix firmly into the joints. This improves the bond. Carefully sweep and dust the bricks before going on to the next step, as any mix that remains may cause stains. (Some staining is usually unavoidable with this method.)

3 Dampening the surface

Using an extremely fine spray, so as not to splash mortar out of the joints, wet down the paving. Don't allow pools to form, and try not to wash away the mortar. Over the next two to three hours, wet the paving periodically, keeping it damp. Tool the joints when the mortar is firm enough. After a few hours, scrub the bricks with burlap to remove mortar stains. For further cleaning instructions, turn to page 182.

Laying bricks in wet mortar

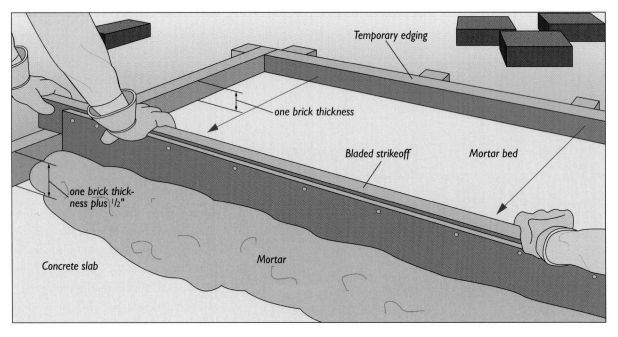

Temporary edging

one brick thickness

Bladed strikeoff

Mortar bed

one brick thickness plus ¹/₂"

Concrete slab

Mortar

1 Placing the mortar bed

Place a ¹/₂"-thick wet-mortar bed between temporary edgings staked against a concrete slab. The edgings are set for the thickness of a brick plus ¹/₂" inch for the mortar. Smooth or shovel the mortar onto the surface with a mason's trowel or square shovel. Strike off the bed with a bladed strikeoff that rides on the edgings and extends down the thickness of one brick. Mix only as much mortar as you can use in an hour, and strike off only about 10 square feet at a time. Get a helper for this step if possible.

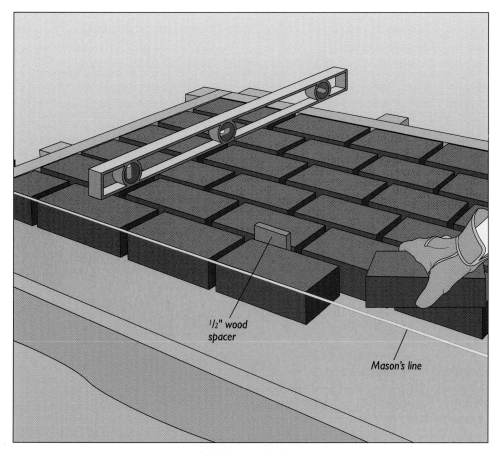

2 Placing the bricks
Place the bricks in your chosen pattern *(page 56)*, leaving ¹/₂" open joints between them (use a wood spacer). Gently tap each one to bed it. Use a mason's line and a level for alignment.

¹/₂" wood spacer

Mason's line

3 Filling the joints
Use a small trowel to pack the mortar—the same mix as the bed—into the joints, working carefully to minimize spilling. Tool the joints with a convex jointer, broom handle, or other convex object. Scrub the paving several hours later with burlap to remove mortar stains.

Building with Concrete Pavers

Concrete pavers offer several advantages to the do-it-yourself homeowner. They are durable, relatively inexpensive, and easy to lay. And, as you can see on page 59, they come in a variety of shapes and sizes.

Interlocking pavers fit together like puzzle pieces. They're available in tan, brown, red, and natural gray, plus blended colors. Some even have holes in them for planting—ideal for grassy parking areas. Unlike pavers made simply of cast concrete, these are cast and then compacted, giving them greater strength.

Interlocking pavers are laid in sand, just like brick; alignment is nearly automatic. Regular (noninterlocking) pavers are also used like brick, but these can be set in either sand or dry mortar. Setting pavers in dry mortar creates a slightly more stable patio and a more formal look than can be achieved with sand.

For a distinctive look that may be just right for your needs, consider casting your own concrete pavers, as described on page 151.

Before you begin, make sure you're familiar with the techniques for working with concrete.

Wood and cast concrete are the most popular edging materials for concrete pavers. If you choose wood, professionals recommend using 2-by-6s instead of 2-by-4s.

Another alternative is plastic edging, which comes in the form of ridged strips for straight edges and kerfed sections for curves. Plastic edgings are set below finished paving height and covered from view with soil.

Cutting Pavers with a Tub Saw

Pavers can be cut to size with a tub saw. Also known as a "wet saw," the blade of a tub saw is kept cool by a stream of running water. Before operating the saw, fill the tray with water and adjust the blade according to the thickness of the paver to be cut. Hold the paver in position, press down, and slowly push the sliding plate forward to feed the paver into the blade. Wear a face shield and keep your hands well away from the blade.

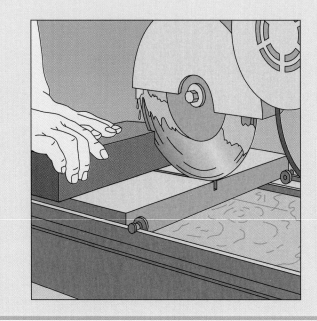

A rented tub saw makes short and neat work of cutting patio paving. In addition to pavers, tub saws can also be used to cut ceramic tiles.

Laying pavers in sand

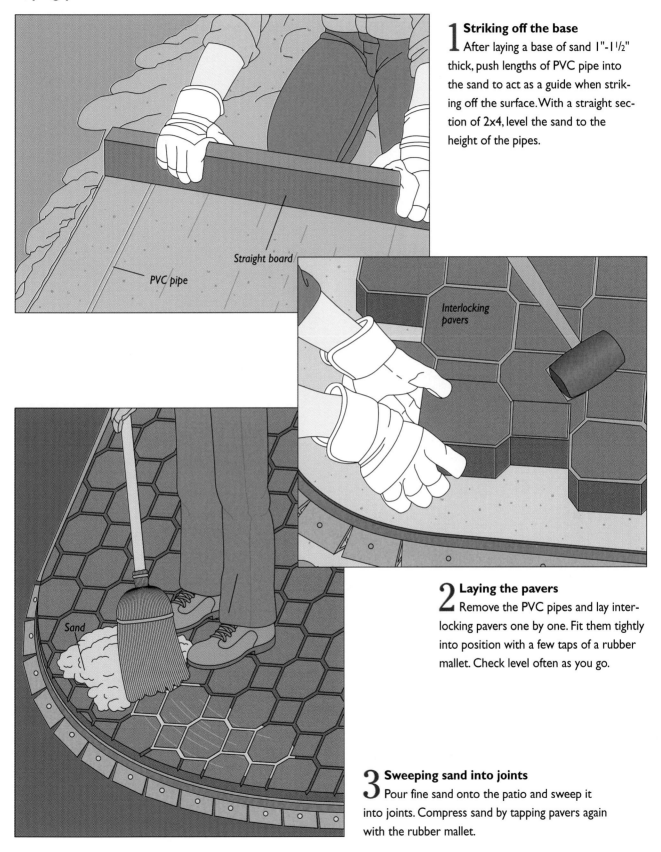

PVC pipe

Straight board

Interlocking pavers

Sand

1 Striking off the base
After laying a base of sand 1"-1½" thick, push lengths of PVC pipe into the sand to act as a guide when striking off the surface. With a straight section of 2x4, level the sand to the height of the pipes.

2 Laying the pavers
Remove the PVC pipes and lay interlocking pavers one by one. Fit them tightly into position with a few taps of a rubber mallet. Check level often as you go.

3 Sweeping sand into joints
Pour fine sand onto the patio and sweep it into joints. Compress sand by tapping pavers again with the rubber mallet.

Laying pavers in dry mortar

1 Laying the pavers
It is crucial to place the units a uniform distance apart. To do this, butt them against a ³/₄" plywood spacer, as shown. Then set them and pack them as for pavers in sand. However, instead of sweeping sand into joints, add a sand-and-cement mortar mix—just as for bricks set in dry mortar.

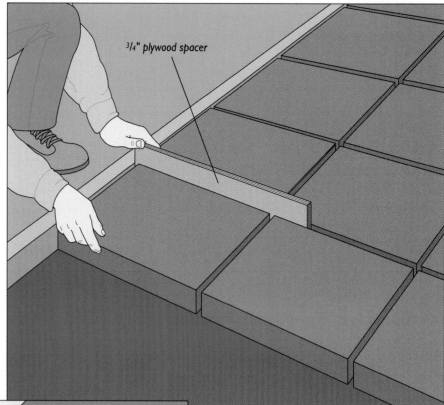

³/₄" plywood spacer

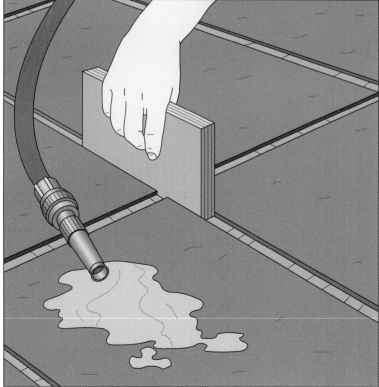

2 Packing the joints
Pack down mortar joints with a piece of wood. Dampen mortar and smooth with a jointer or similar tool to improve the finished appearance. Expect some discoloration in the finished product.

Casting your own pavers

1 Digging and filling the hole

Dig a hole about 4" deep for each "stone," contouring it as you like but keeping the sides close to vertical. For easy walking, space the steps no more than 18" from the center of one to the center of the next. On a lawn, plan to keep the tops of the stones below grade to allow for mowing. Use a basic concrete mix *(page 165)* to fill the holes.

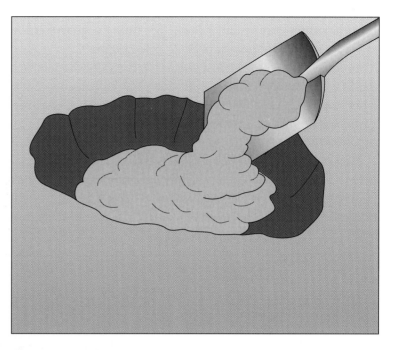

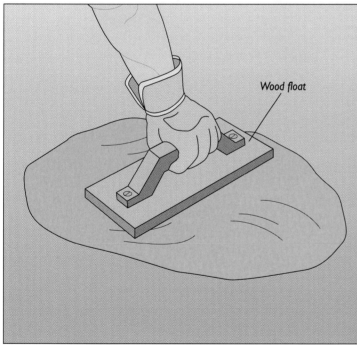

Wood float

2 Finishing the stones

Finish the stones with a wood float or a magnesium hand float. Cover and cure them as described for a concrete slab on page 171. You might want to try the travertine texture *(page 174)* to enhance the overall appearance. The finished pathway should have an easy, natural look.

Building Stone Patios

Natural stone—cut or uncut flagstone, rough cobbles, and the like—looks pleasant in almost any garden setting. Its natural, unfinished appearance blends well with garden plants, and its subdued color adds warmth.

Stone's primary drawback is that it can cost up to five times as much as brick or concrete. Geography often dictates price: the farther you are from the quarry, the higher the price will be.

Irregularly shaped flagstone can be laid in firm soil, in a sand bed, or in mortar (over either sand or concrete). In northern climates it is recommended that flagstone be set in mortar over a concrete slab. This reduces heaving caused by extreme changes in temperature and limits settling. Flagstone is also available precut to rectangular shapes; these tighter-fitting pieces work well laid in a bed of sand *(page 155)*.

For the look of stone at a lower price, river rock and fieldstone are two rustic alternatives. Depending on stone size and the effect desired, you can "seed" them into concrete or place them individually in mortar or in a concrete setting bed.

Cutting Flagstone

Since flagstones are generally irregularly shaped, you'll need to fit and cut most pieces before setting them in place. To cut or trim a stone, lap the neighboring stone over the stone to be cut and trace its outline. Next, score the outline with a brickset. Place a length of wood under the stone so that the waste portion and the scored line overhang it, as shown below. Strike sharply along the scored line with a brickset and soft-headed hammer or a mallet. Remember to wear eye protection.

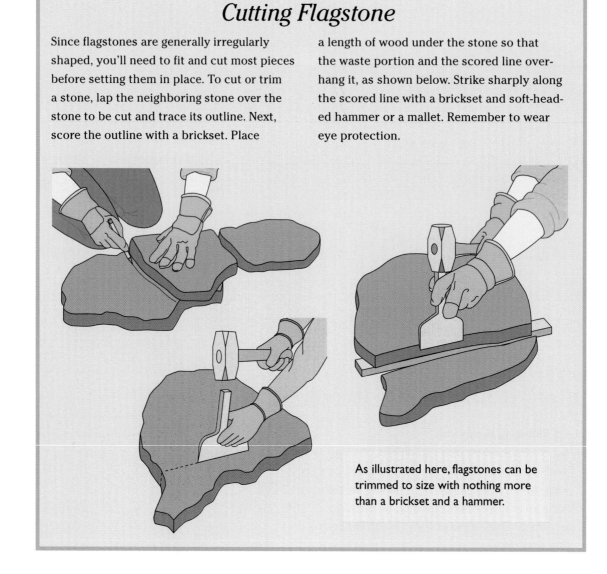

As illustrated here, flagstones can be trimmed to size with nothing more than a brickset and a hammer.

Laying flagstone in mortar

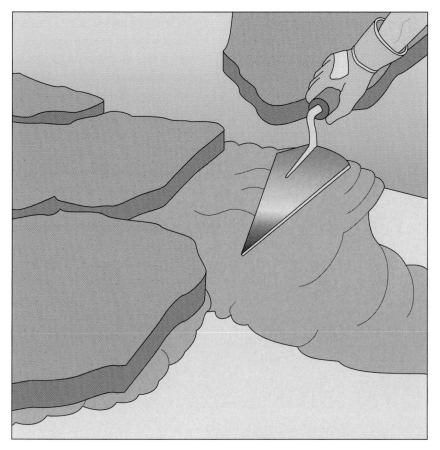

1 Laying flagstone

Lay a slab that is reinforced with wire mesh *(page 167)*. While the concrete is still plastic, scratch the surface with a folded piece of hardware cloth to provide "tooth" for the mortar. Once the slab is dry, arrange the stones, cutting and trimming them as necessary for a close fit.

Next, prepare a 1:3 portland cement mixture, enough to cover 10 to 12 square feet. At the same time, prepare a second "heavy-cream" mixture, or slurry, of portland cement and water.

Starting in a corner, spread enough of the thicker mortar to make a full bed for one or two stones, varying the thickness of the bed to make up for the variations in stone thickness. Furrow the mortar with your trowel. Before setting the stones back in place, butter the bottom of each one with the slurry.

2 Bedding the stones

Set each stone firmly in place, bedding it with a rubber mallet. Align the edges of the outer stones with the perimeter of the slab or let them overhang it slightly.

To maintain an even surface, use a straightedge and level. If a stone isn't level, lift it up and scoop out or add mortar as needed. Butter the bottom of the stone with the slurry, lay it back down and tap it into place.

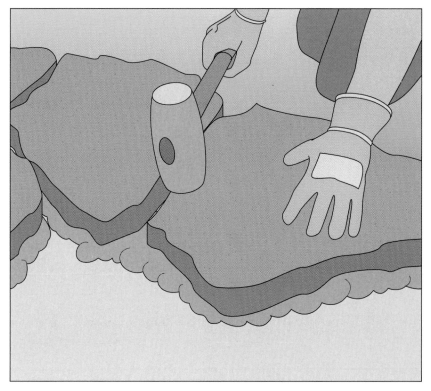

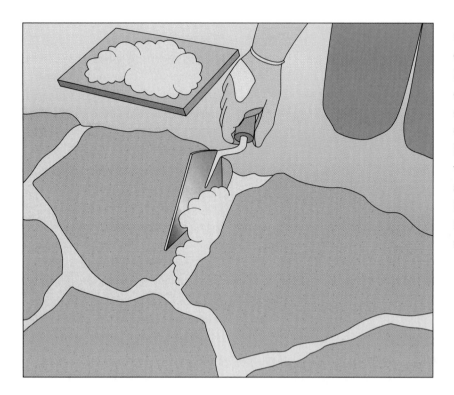

3 Filling the joints
Let the mortar set overnight. Prepare a mixture of one part portland cement to three parts mortar sand, and enough water to produce a good troweling consistency. Pack the mortar between the stones. Smooth the joints with a pointing trowel, and clean up spills with a sponge, water and household cleaner. A weak 1 to 10 solution of muriatic acid and water also may be used, but never on limestone or marble.

Laying a Flagstone Path

If you want to lay a paved garden path in a hurry, flagstone may be just what you need. Flagstones can be placed in a stepping-stone pattern over a layer of gravel and sand— with no digging required.

In addition to being quick and easy to lay, flagstone blends in well with virtually all other patio pavings, making it an ideal secondary material in a larger patio design.

The simple flagstone path at left offers easy access to this garden. Flagstone is an easy material to work with as it often requires no excavation to lay.

Laying rectangular stones in sand

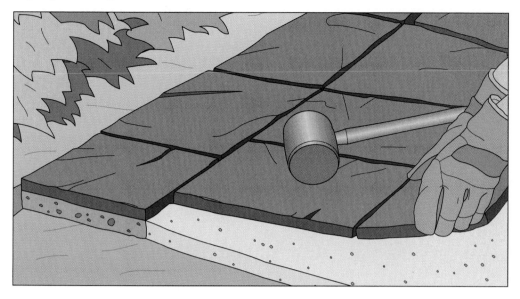

Laying down the stones

Install invisible edgings the width of the rectangular stones. As when laying bricks in sand, lay stones in a tight pattern. Bed each unit by tapping lightly with a mallet and check progress with a level. Scoop out or fill sand to compensate for variations in stone thickness. Sweep additional dry sand into joints to lock units together.

Setting a mosaic in mortar

1 Setting the stones
Prepare a 1:3 cement-mortar sand mixture and spread it over a concrete slab to a depth of ½". Spread only as much mortar as you can fill with stones in an hour. Cut the dry edges away from the previous mortar bed before spreading the next section. Keep the stones in a pail of water, setting them in the mortar while they're still wet.

Push the stones deep enough that the mortar gets a good hold on them—generally just past the middle.

2 Leveling the stones

Use a straight board to level the stones. Let the mortar set for an hour or two, then spread a thin layer of mortar over the surface and into the gaps. Hose and brush off the excess before it sets.

Laying fieldstone in concrete

Placing the stones

Cast the slab but don't completely fill the forms. Push the stones into the concrete one by one, covering slightly more than half the stone. When the concrete has hardened somewhat, expose the stones as desired by carefully brushing the concrete while dampening the surface with a fine spray.

Building Adobe Patios

It's hard to match adobe for friendly, rustic charm. And because the pavers are large, construction generally goes quickly.

Adobe blocks can be quite heavy, so be careful when lifting them and, ideally, enlist a helper.

It's best to lay adobe in sand, which allows for good drainage and extends the life of the blocks. The procedure is essentially the same as for other masonry units (brick, stone, etc.), with a few important differences. With adobe, edgings are not always necessary,

especially if the surface of the finished paving will be at ground level. You can just pack surrounding soil against the edges of the area to retain the pavers. Of course, if you choose to use an edging you can have the surface of the paving slightly above ground level. Some of the many edging options are shown below.

With adobe, it's even more important than with other paving units that the sand bed be level: If blocks straddle humps or bridge hollows, they're more likely to crack.

Adobe blocks can be set in patterns, just as other masonry units can. Running bond, jack-on-jack, and basket weave all work well; the latter two possibilities reduce the number of cut blocks. Illustrations of possible bond patterns can be found starting on page 56. If you do need to cut adobe, try an old handsaw, or a hammer and brickset.

It's best to leave one-inch open joints, to compensate for irregularities in block sizes and shapes. You can fill the joints with sand or soil and plantings, for a softer look.

Borders for Your Adobe

Of course, any edging that's appropriate for brick, stone, or tile patios is a possibility for adobe. But some choices seem especially suited. Wood edgings, for example, harmonize well with adobe's rustic look. Pressure-treated landscape timbers have the added

advantage of complementing the bulk of the adobe blocks. And even adobe can be a border for adobe. You can make an invisible edging by setting blocks in a narrow foundation of concrete *(page 140)*, or set the edging block on a larger adobe block for support.

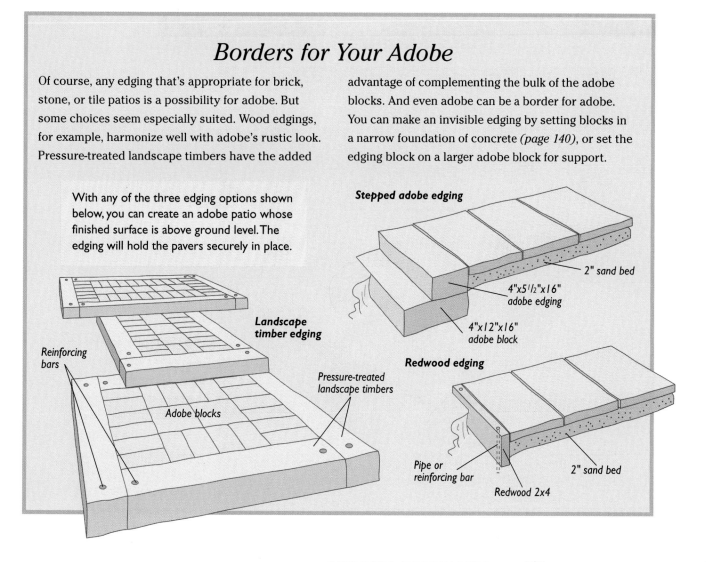

With any of the three edging options shown below, you can create an adobe patio whose finished surface is above ground level. The edging will hold the pavers securely in place.

Reinforcing bars

Adobe blocks

Landscape timber edging

Pressure-treated landscape timbers

Stepped adobe edging

2" sand bed

4"x5¹/₂"x16" adobe edging

4"x12"x16" adobe block

Redwood edging

Pipe or reinforcing bar

Redwood 2x4

2" sand bed

Laying adobe in sand

1 Placing the adobe
Strike off and level a 2" sand bed. Set the blocks on the sand, spacing them about 1" apart. Scoop out or fill in sand under individual blocks as necessary to compensate for irregularities in thickness. Work from a 2' square of plywood to keep from disturbing the sand bed.

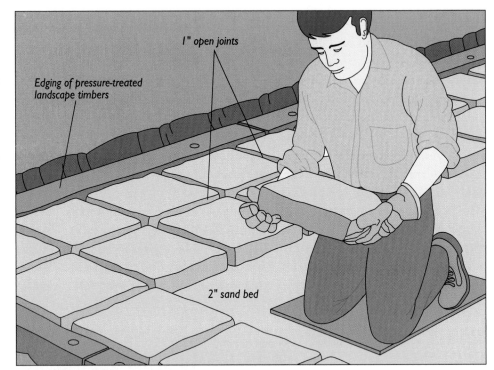

1" open joints

Edging of pressure-treated landscape timbers

2" sand bed

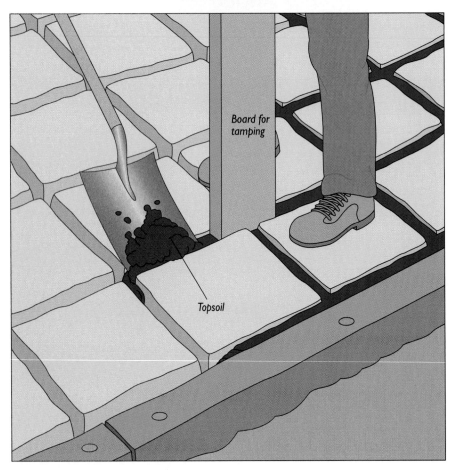

Board for tamping

Topsoil

2 Filling the joints
With a helper, shovel topsoil into the spaces between the blocks and pack it in place with the end of a board. To soften the look of the patio, add low-growing plants that spread to the topsoil after all the joints have been filled.

Building Tile Patios

Terra-cotta tiles make an attractive, long-lasting patio. Laying tile outdoors is within the capabilities of the do-it-yourselfer, but you'll need to plan carefully; even small flaws in installation may be noticeable in the finished patio. Perhaps the most crucial element in preparation for tile is proper preparation of the subsurface on which the tile will be laid. If it is not perfectly flat, the finished tiles won't be either.

Sand is not a stable base for tile; choose the wet mortar method over a mesh-reinforced concrete slab instead. Either tile over an existing concrete slab, or cast a new one. For concrete basics, see page 164.

Tile Cutting Techniques

If a lot of tiles must be cut to complete a pattern or fill in an oddly shaped space, it's easiest to mark the cutting lines and have them sawn at a masonry yard equipped with a diamond-bladed saw. Otherwise, you can rent a tile saw (also called a tub saw) to do the task yourself. The blade you'll need depends on the tile to be cut, so take a sample of the tile with you to the rental store so you get the appropriate blade. If you have only a few cuts, a portable circular saw with a masonry-cutting blade or a snap cutter, which can be rented from a tile dealer, will also do the job. Use tile nippers for irregular shapes, first marking the cutting line by scoring with a small glass cutter.

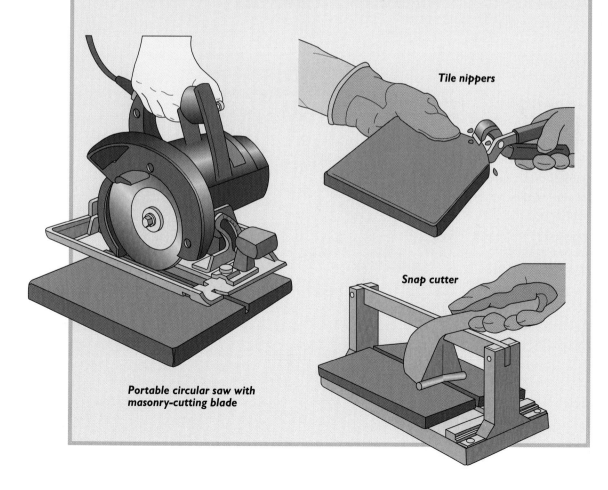

Tile nippers

Snap cutter

Portable circular saw with masonry-cutting blade

Laying tile in wet mortar

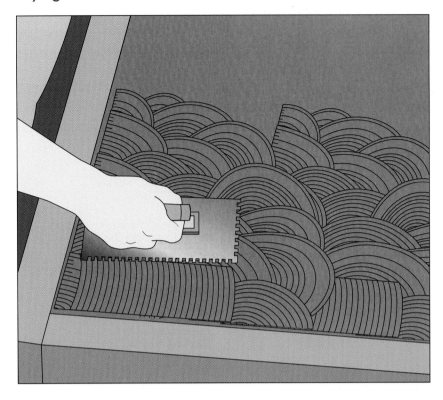

1 Applying the mortar bed
If you're using an existing slab, wash it with a diluted muriatic acid solution, then clean it and rinse well. Purchase thin-set mortar mix for tile setting and mix it to a smooth paste consistency according to label instructions.

Install permanent or temporary edgings; they should rise above the concrete slab one tile thickness plus 1/2" for the mortar bed. Use the flat side of a recommended trowel to spread the mortar, working in 8'-10' squares at a time. Comb the mortar with the notched side of the trowel, holding it at a 45° angle to the slab.

2 Placing the tiles
Beginning in one corner, set the tiles in place, leaving 1/2" open joints. To ensure proper spacing and alignment, use 1/2" thick pieces of plywood or molded plastic spacers. Press the tiles down slightly, ensuring that the mortar doesn't come up more than one-third of the way into the joints.

Let tiles set for 24 hours before filling the joints with grout *(step 3)*.

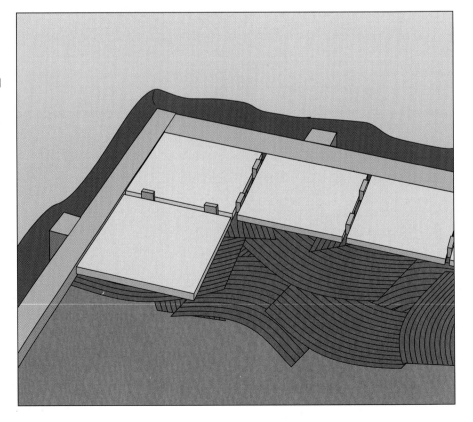

3 Filling the joints

Once the mortar is dry, fill the joints between the tiles using commercial tile grout. Mix the grout according to the instructions and work it into the joints using a rubber grout float held at 30° *(left)*. Force grout into the joints so they are completely filled; check that there are no air pockets.

Cement-sand grout

4 Cleaning the surface

Scrape off the excess grout with the rubber-backed trowel held at 45°. Work diagonally to avoid disturbing the joints. Clean off the trowel frequently in a bucket of water. Let the grout set for 15 minutes before cleaning. Once it dries, wipe off any film with a soft, clean cloth. If a latex additive was added to the grout and mortar during mixing, damp-curing the tiles is unnecessary. Otherwise, keep the tiles damp for approximately one week.

Working with Loose Materials

Patios and walkways made with loose materials are economical, easy to install, and look good combined with other patio materials.

Careful preparation is the key to a first-rate job. Prepare the site *(page 132)* and install edgings to keep the material in bounds. A grid of 2-by-4 dividers within large paved areas will help keep the paving evenly distributed. Use geotextile fabric under the paving to deter weeds (it won't hinder drainage). All loose materials are best laid over a 1-inch-thick compacted base of decomposed granite or construction sand, available from your supplier.

You'll need a wheelbarrow and an iron rake for hauling and spreading, and a large drum roller to pack both the base and the surface material; the wheelbarrow and drum roller can be rented.

Gravel: Particularly effective in low-traffic areas, gravel provides a low-cost, fast-draining surface. Once installed, as described below, gravel requires little care. Pea gravel can be raked to remove leaves or maintain desired patterns; larger gravels can be cleaned with a leaf blower or vacuum. You may need to renew the surface every few years.

Bark: A by-product of the lumber industry, bark is available in a variety of sizes. Choose the one that gives the effect you want. Lay it 2 to 4 inches thick on the prepared base. Finely shredded redwood bark (gorilla hair) makes a natural-looking top dressing. You can add it to the bark, or use it alone over crushed rock or decomposed granite.

Decomposed granite and crushed rock: Because particle sizes range from sand to quite large pieces of rock, decomposed granite and crushed rock make good pavings that pack tightly together and don't move underfoot.

Lay these materials over the prepared site in the same way as for the decomposed granite base for gravel *(below)*. In this case, however, plan to build up a 2½- to 4-inch-thick paving in 1-inch increments.

Redrock: Because redrock isn't always graded by size, you may need a ¼-inch mesh sieve to sift out enough fine material to set aside for a ¾-inch-thick topping.

After preparing the base, lay and level a 2½- to 4-inch-thick layer of the larger material, building it up in 1-inch increments, wetting it down, and rolling it with a drum roller. Finally, distribute the sifted material evenly over the base, dampening and rolling once more.

Laying down gravel

1 Applying the base
Install edgings, making sure they extend high enough above the ground to contain the paving at its finished thickness, then lay down sheets of geotextile fabric. Bring wheelbarrow loads of decomposed granite *(left)* or sand to the site, distributing them as evenly as possible over the area.

2 Raking the base

Have a helper wet the decomposed granite or sand with a fine spray from a hose while you rake it evenly over the site. Fill any hollows and level high spots until the base forms a uniform 1" thick layer.

3 Rolling the base

Using a drum roller, roll the wet base several times to pack it evenly. A firm base helps keep the gravel topcoat from "traveling" when you walk on it.

4 Applying the surface material

Spread gravel 2-3" thick and rake it evenly over the base. (Coverage varies with size and weight, but generally you'll need about 1 1/2 tons of rock to cover 100 sq. ft.) Roll the surface several times to compress the gravel and lock it into place.

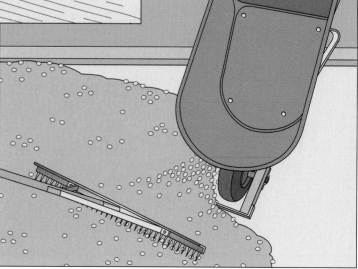

Casting Concrete Patios

Concrete is practical, serviceable, versatile, and fairly economical. With it, you can create anything from small stepping-stones to sizable patios. Concrete makes attractive walkways and combines well with other paving materials, such as brick or tile.

On a small scale, concrete is relatively easy to work with. But casting an entire patio can be a daunting job. It is possible to create an attractive patio yourself, but careful planning and preparation is essential. It's best to place all the concrete at once; a large area can be divided into manageable sections using 2-by-4s.

Preparing the site, building and installing forms, preparing the base, and adding any necessary rein-forcement—and even placing the concrete—are manageable jobs, even for novices, but finishing concrete takes skill and experience. Once concrete is in place, you're stuck with it; repair or replacement is costly and difficult.

For this reason, many people prefer to hire a professional, who will have the skills, the assistants, and the equipment required to create a solid, long-lasting slab. Professionals also offer attractive surface treatments, such as stamping, that are more difficult for a do-it-yourselfer.

Casting a slab that will be the base for another patio surface material, however, is a task that even a less-experienced do-it-yourselfer can tackle with confidence. Careful plan-ning is still required, but irregularities in the finished slab will be hidden under the surface material. Remember to calculate the thickness of the surface material when you're excavating the site.

When a new concrete patio abuts existing concrete, such as the house foundation, an isolation joint is required, to let both structures move independently. Fasten 1/2-inch-thick 4-inch-wide asphalt-impregnated isolation-joint strips against the existing structure before casting the concrete. A 2-by-4 against, but not fastened to, the house, as shown below, can serve the same function and is a good choice if you're using permanent wood forms. It also acts as a permanent fourth form.

ANATOMY OF A PATIO

If the slab is to be used as the base for tile, pavers, or another surface material, use 6" square welded-wire mesh to hold the cracks tightly together. Otherwise, wooden dividers, as shown here, or control joints cut into the freshly cast concrete *(page 170)*, provide a means of directing the cracks.

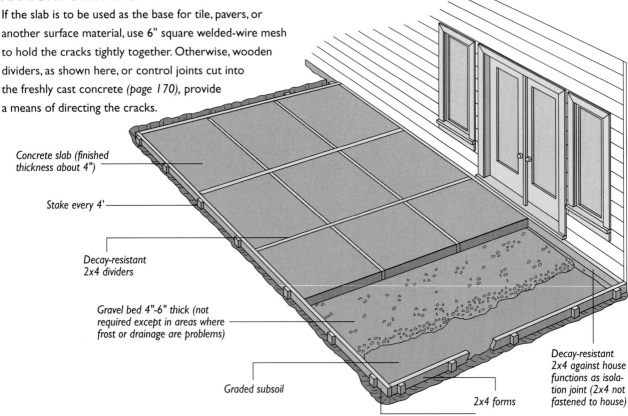

Concrete slab (finished thickness about 4")

Stake every 4'

Decay-resistant 2x4 dividers

Gravel bed 4"-6" thick (not required except in areas where frost or drainage are problems)

Graded subsoil

2x4 forms

Decay-resistant 2x4 against house functions as isolation joint (2x4 not fastened to house)

The following concrete formula will give you good results for most residential paving projects. Choose either the basic mix or, for freezing climates, the one that contains an air-entraining agent.

Basic concrete formula: All proportions are by volume and based on the use of $3/4$-inch coarse aggregate (stone).

>1 part portland cement
>$2^1/2$ parts sand
>$2^1/2$ parts aggregate
>$1/2$ part water

Air-entrained concrete: Adding an air-entraining agent—a liquid compound that creates microscopic air bubbles in the finished concrete—helps concrete resist freeze-thaw damage in colder regions. The agent also makes concrete more workable and easier to finish. The extra workability means you can add less water to a batch, making the finished concrete stronger. For this reason, an air-entraining agent should be used with ready-mix, whatever the local climate. Specify this when you place your order. The amount of agent you need will vary by brand, so consult your supplier. If you're using an agent, reduce the sand to $2^1/4$ parts. Air-entrained concrete must be mixed with a power mixer and finished with a metal float.

Always use clean construction sand, not beach sand. The aggregate should range from quite small to about $3/4$ inch in size. The water should be drinkable—neither excessively alkaline nor acidic, and containing absolutely no organic matter.

To determine how much concrete you need to buy, refer to the table below. The figures given are for 30 square feet of finished 4-inch-thick concrete slab and include 10% extra for waste.

INGREDIENTS FOR A 30-SQUARE-FOOT SLAB (4 INCHES THICK)	
MATERIAL	**AMOUNT**
Bulk dry material	Portland cement: 3 sacks Sand: 7.5 cubic feet Aggregate (gravel): 7.5 cubic feet
Dry pre-packaged mix	Twenty-five 60-pound sacks
Ready-mix	$1/2$ cubic yard

TWO FORM OPTIONS

Forms for concrete patios are essentially like wood edgings. They may be temporary—removed when the job is done, or permanent. In either case, they must be fastened securely and staked every 4 feet to withstand the force of the concrete. Temporary forms should be coated with a commercial form-release agent to aid in stripping.

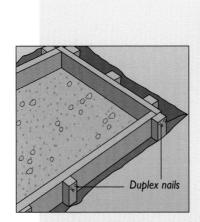

Duplex nails

Temporary forms
Fasten forms securely to stakes using duplex nails. These nails, which have a second head, hold strongly enough to withstand the pressure of the plastic concrete, but are easier to remove when stripping forms. Rot-resistant wood is not necessary, since it won't be a permanent part of the finished structure.

$3^1/2$" galvanized nails
Rot-resistant 2x4
Beveled stakes

Permanent forms
Use rot-resistant wood for the forms, fastening them securely to the stakes with galvanized nails. Drive $3^1/2$" galvanized nails part-way into the form from the inside, about every 16"; this will lock the form to the slab. Stakes on the outside of the forms are beveled so they can be covered with earth.

Mixing concrete

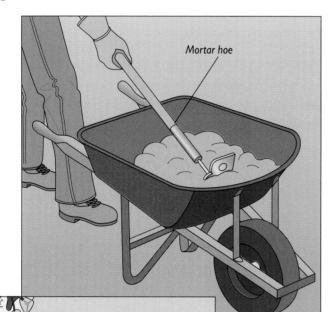

Mortar hoe

Using a mortar hoe

To work with 1 to 2 cubic feet of concrete at a time, use a high-sided wheelbarrow *(left)* or a homemade or commercial mortar box. Use a shovel to measure ingredients—it's accurate enough if your shovelsful are consistent; use a container of known volume to determine the approximate volume of a shovelful. Mark a bucket off in quarts and gallons for the water.

First, place the sand on the mixing surface and add the cement, mixing well with a mortar hoe; add the gravel and mix again. Next, mound up the mixture and hollow out the center to form a well, then pour in the water. Work around the hollow, pulling dry ingredients into the water to enlarge the well. Keep mixing until the blend is uniform in color.

Using a concrete mixer

You can rent, borrow, or buy concrete mixers in sizes ranging from $\frac{1}{2}$ to 7 cubic foot capacity, but the smaller ones (less than 3 cubic feet) don't pay off. A mixer can be electric or gas powered. Set the mixer close to your sand and gravel piles so that you can shovel-feed directly. Be sure the mixer is level and chock (wedge) it in place to prevent "walking." Concrete mixers can be dangerous; read the safety information opposite.

To mix ingredients, add half the water and all the coarse aggregate with the mixer off. Then, turn it on (warm it up if it's gas powered) to scour the drum. Measuring your ingredients by equal shovelsful, and throwing them from outside the drum, add all of the sand, along with all but the last 10% of the water. Next, add the portland cement. When the mixture is a uniform color and texture, add the rest of the water and the air-entraining agent, if you're using one. You can purchase air-entraining agent at some haul-it-yourself concrete dealers. Several brands are available. Ask the dealer for use instructions for the brand he carries. After adding the final ingredients, mix for at least 2 minutes to get a uniform appearance.

TESTING A TRIAL BATCH

Work a sample of your first batch with a mason's trowel. The concrete should slide—not run—freely off the trowel. You should be able to smooth the surface fairly easily, so that the large aggregate is submerged. All of the aggregate at the edges of the sample should be completely and evenly coated with cement.

If your mix is too stiff, add a little water. If it's too wet and soupy, add some sand-cement mixture, proportioned according to your recipe. If you do make adjustments to a recipe, record the changes accurately so you can incorporate them in the next batch.

Working Safely with a Concrete Mixer

Be sure to follow all safety measures recommended for the mixer you're using. Never reach into a rotating mixer drum with your hands or tools. Always throw the ingredients in from outside the drum. Wear tight-fitting clothes, a dust mask, and goggles, and keep well away from the moving parts. Do not look into the mixer while it's running—check the mix by dumping a little out.

To avoid shock hazard, an electric mixer must be plugged into a ground-fault circuit interrupter-protected outlet. It needs a three-prong grounding-type plug and an outdoor-rated three-wire extension cord. Do not run an electric mixer in wet or damp conditions and be sure to cover it with a tarpaulin when not in use. The engine on a gas-powered mixer should be fueled

from a proper can for storing and pouring flammable fuel. Add fuel only when the engine is stopped and cooled off. Any fuel spills should be cleaned up immediately. Be sure to close the fuel container tightly after each fueling. While the engine is running, don't work or stand where you must breathe the exhaust fumes. Never run the mixer in an enclosed space.

Casting a concrete slab

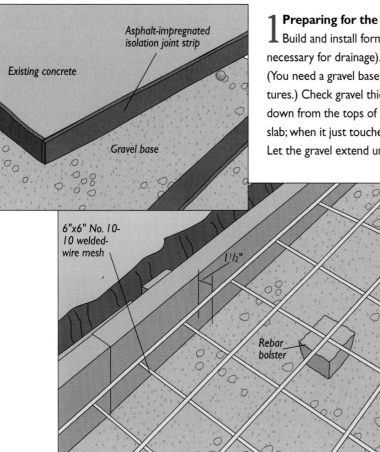

Asphalt-impregnated isolation joint strip

Existing concrete

Gravel base

6"x6" No. 10-10 welded-wire mesh

1 1/2"

Rebar bolster

1 Preparing for the casting

Build and install forms, making sure they're level (or properly graded, if necessary for drainage). Place and level a 4"-6" bed of gravel, if necessary. (You need a gravel base in areas of poor drainage or freezing temperatures.) Check gravel thickness with a homemade template that extends down from the tops of the forms the desired thickness of the finished slab; when it just touches the top of the gravel, the base is thick enough. Let the gravel extend under the edges of the forms.

If the slab will abut an existing slab or structure, install isolation-joint strips. Attach the strips flush with the top of an existing slab using hardened concrete nails or construction adhesive.

If you'll be topping the slab with mortared paving units like bricks, you won't be able to use control joints, so reinforcing mesh is recommended to hold the cracks together when they occur. Use 6" square No. 10-10 welded-wire mesh and use rebar bolsters or pieces of block to hold the mesh midway in the slab and at least 1 1/2" from the sides of the forms. Cut the mesh with bolt cutters or heavy pliers.

Working Safely with Concrete

Always wear safety goggles when working with concrete. Plastic concrete is caustic, so wear gloves to protect your hands. Also, wear rubber boots if you're going to have to walk in the concrete to strike it off. If plastic concrete comes in contact with your skin—including through clothing—wash thoroughly with water.

2 Placing the concrete
Thoroughly dampen the soil or gravel. Start placing the concrete at one corner of the form while a helper uses a shovel or hoe to spread it *(above)*.

Work the concrete up against the form and compact it into all corners with a square shovel or mortar hoe; with a hoe, push—don't drag—the concrete. But don't overwork the concrete, and don't spread it too far; overworking will force the heavy aggregate to the bottom of the slab and will bring up small particles that can cause defects in the finished concrete. Instead, space out your placement along the form, placing each batch against the previous batch to fill the form.

If you plan to leave the dividers in, place, finish, and cure the concrete in alternating sections. (Imagine it like a checkerboard and do all the red squares first.) Once they've cured for at least three days, remove the stakes from inside of the remaining sections (black squares) and complete them.

3 Striking the concrete
Move a strikeoff (in this case, a straight 2x4) across the form to level the concrete. On large jobs, do this batch-by-batch, rather than after all the concrete is placed. Move the board slowly along the form, using a zigzag, sawing motion; make two passes. Even on narrow forms, two people will make the work faster and more accurate. A third person can shovel extra concrete into any hollows.

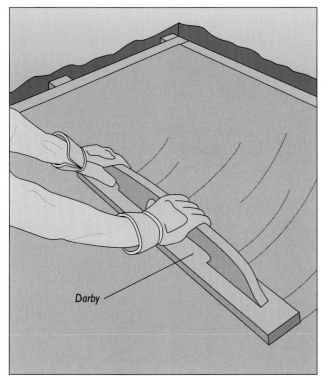

Darby

Bull float

4 Initial smoothing

(On very small projects, you can skip this step.) After striking off, use a darby or bull float—depending on the size of your project—for the initial finishing, to smooth down high spots and fill small hollows left after striking off.

Use the darby (above, left) on small projects. Move it in overlapping arcs, then repeat with overlapping straight, side-to-side strokes. Keep the tool flat, but don't let it dig in.

For larger jobs, use a bull float (above, right). Push it away from you with its leading edge raised slightly. Pull it back nearly flat; overlap your passes.

Place and finish the remaining sections of the slab following steps 1 to 4.

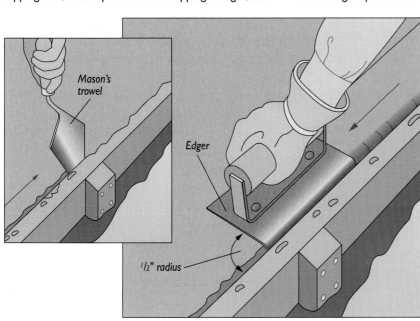

Mason's trowel

Edger

¹/₂" radius

5 Edging

Giving the concrete a smoothly curved edge will help it resist chipping. To edge the concrete, begin by running a mason's trowel between the concrete and the outer edges of the slab form (inset). Follow with an edger (left). Run it back and forth to smooth and compact the concrete. Unless the tool has a toboggan end, raise the leading edge slightly as you move it.

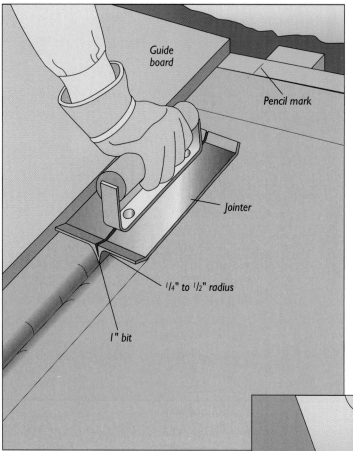

Guide board

Pencil mark

Jointer

1/4" to 1/2" radius

1" bit

6 Jointing

Use a 1" deep jointer with a straight guide board to make control joints *(left)*. You can kneel on this board to reach the middle of a wide slab. Depth of control joints should be one-quarter of the slab's thickness. Control joints can be made at intervals of about 1 1/2 times the width of the slab but the distance between them should not exceed 30 times the thickness of the slab—10' for a 4" slab. For concrete made using 3/4" coarse aggregate, reduce the maximum control joint spacing to 8' for a 4" slab. Jointed sections should never be more than 1 1/2 times as long as they are wide. Measure along the forms to locate the joints and mark them with a pencil. The edging and jointing marks may be left or removed by floating.

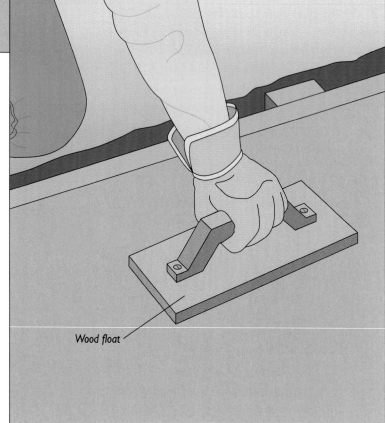

Wood float

7 Floating and troweling

After the water sheen has disappeared from the concrete, but before the surface has become really stiff, float with a wood float or a magnesium hand float. The latter gives a smoother surface. With air-entrained concrete, use a magnesium float—a wood float can tear the surface. With both types of float, hold the tool flat on the surface. To reach the middle of a large slab, kneel on boards and then finish over the board marks as you work backwards.

Unless you are going to broom-finish them afterward, don't use a steel trowel on outdoor surfaces, it creates a very slick surface that can be dangerous when wet.

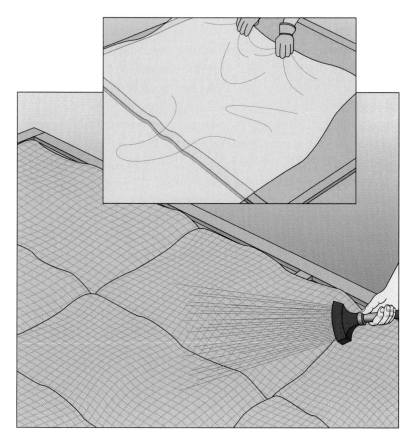

8 Curing the slab

Slabs need to be moist cured to keep their surfaces from drying too quickly. If the surface dries too soon, it will be weak and may later become powdery or crumble away. Cure your concrete by keeping it wet. Cover the slab with burlap, sand, straw, or other material and wet it (left). Wet it down as needed until curing is finished.

Another option is to use plastic sheeting (inset) or a commercial curing compound. Water evaporating from the slab will be trapped, eliminating the need for wetting.

Whatever method you choose, curing should last a minimum of three days—longer in cold weather—but it's best to let the slab cure for a week, just to be on the safe side.

Installing Supports

If your patio plan includes an overhead, you can embed supports for its posts directly in the plastic concrete. U-shaped post bases offer the best support and are recommended for freestanding overheads. You work the bases down into the freshly placed concrete as soon as the concrete is firm enough to hold them after initial smoothing (step 6); if the bases sink, wait for the concrete to firm up a bit more. For final smoothing, you'll have to work around the post bases. Set the bases about 1 inch in from the edges of the slabs. For posts at corners, measure in from the forms on both sides; for intermediate posts, stretch a string guide across the forms at the appropriate position and align the edges of the post bases with it. Level the bases across the tops of the flanges. For attaching overheads to existing slabs, see page 89.

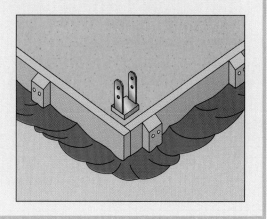

Finishes for Cast Concrete

One of the advantages of cast concrete is that it can take on a number of different looks, depending on the surface treatment applied. Some tasks, such as stamping, are best left to professionals. Others, such as exposing aggregate, creating a rock salt or travertine finish, tooling, and coloring, are potential projects for the skilled do-it-yourselfer, especially on small patio surfaces and walkways, as shown below.

You can, of course, have a professional do these for you as well. Sometimes, it's worth paying a professional to do the job, not because the work itself is difficult, but because a professional will have the experience necessary to know what combination of these techniques is required to produce the look you want. For example, an experienced contractor should be able to choose the appropriate color and tooling pattern to make your concrete slab resemble stone.

Exposed aggregate: The attractive exposed aggregate finish is probably the most common for residential concrete work. There are two ways to produce it: seeding aggregate or large varicolored smooth pebbles into the concrete surface (as described below) or exposing the regular sharp aggregate already in the concrete. To expose the regular aggregate, cast and finish the concrete through the floating stage, being careful not to push the aggregate too deep when floating. Then follow step 3 opposite.

Salt finish: Coarse rock salt can be used for a distinctive pocked surface on concrete, but it's not recommended for areas with severe freezing weather, since water trapped in the pockets will expand upon freezing and crack or chip the surface.

Travertine finish: For a marbled effect, try the travertine finish *(page 174)*. This finish is not recommended in severe freezing climates.

Tooling: Create simulated flagstone by tooling the cast concrete with a convex jointer *(page 174)*.

Coloring: To color concrete you can mix the pigment into the concrete before it's cast, dust a dry-shake color mixture onto a freshly cast slab, or paint on an organic masonry stain. Intensify mixed-in colors by substituting white portland cement for gray. Painted-on pigment is the least durable and will need periodic recoating *(page 175)*.

Seeding aggregate

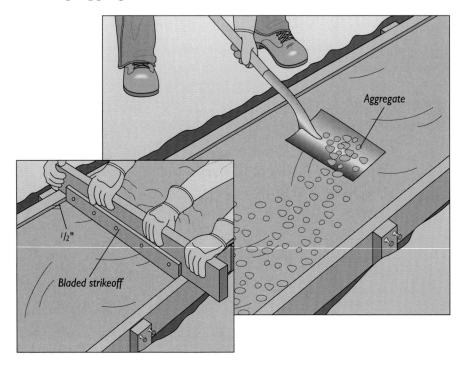

1 Seeding the aggregate
After casting the slab, strike it off about 1/2" below the tops of the form boards using a bladed strike-off *(inset)*.

Using a square shovel, distribute the aggregate evenly over the slab in a single layer *(left)*.

Aggregate

1/2"

Bladed strikeoff

2 Floating

Using a darby, a piece of wood, or a float, press the aggregate down until it lies just below the surface of the concrete *(right)*. Then refloat the surface with a magnesium hand float.

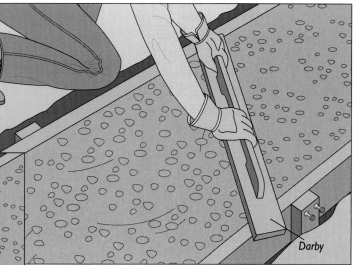

Darby

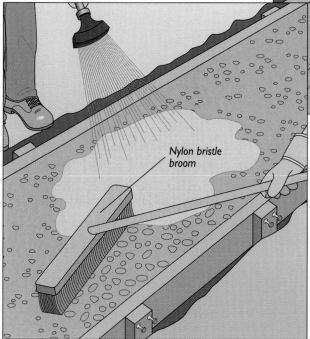

Nylon bristle broom

3 Exposing the aggregate

Expose a small section of aggregate by gently brushing the concrete with a nylon bristle brush while a helper wets the surface with a fine spray of water. If the cement runs, the surface is not ready. If you need to scrub aggressively, it's becoming too hard and you should work quickly to finish the job. Ideally, the combination of light pressure and water will expose the aggregate. Stop brushing when the tops of the stones show *(left)*.

Take care in curing exposed aggregate surfaces; the bond to the aggregate must be strong. After curing, you can remove any cement haze on the stones with a 10% solution of muriatic acid.

Using rock salt

Scatter coarse rock salt sparingly over the surface of floated concrete *(near right)*; embed it using a wood float or a piece of wood *(far right)*. Smooth the surface with either a wood or magnesium hand float.

After curing the concrete, wash out the salt with a strong spray of water from a hose.

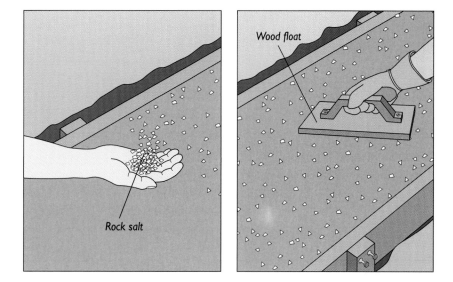

Wood float

Rock salt

Applying a travertine finish

1 Brushing on mortar
After striking off, initial smoothing, and floating, roughen the surface slightly with a broom—or leave it roughly floated. Using a large brush, dash a 1:2 cement-sand mixture unevenly over the surface *(right)*. Coloring the mixture to contrast with the concrete heightens the effect.

Wallpaper or dash brush

Steel trowel

2 Troweling the mortar
When the slab can support you on knee boards, trowel the surface, knocking down high spots *(left)*. The result is a stony texture, smooth on the high spots and rougher in the low spots. Cure the concrete as usual.

Imitating flagstone

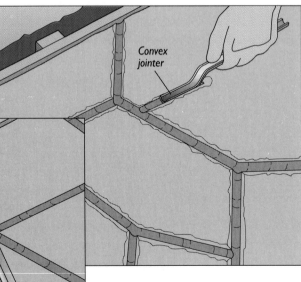

Convex jointer

1 Tooling the surface
Tool the concrete immediately after striking off and floating. Use a convex jointer *(left)* or bend a short length of $1/2$" or $3/4$" copper pipe to make a tool for the task. Sketch your pattern in advance and work from the plan. Erasures are awkward, so you need a sure hand.

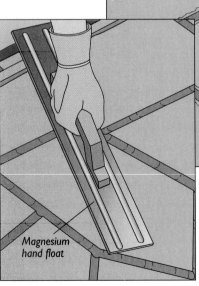

Magnesium hand float

2 Floating
When the water sheen has disappeared, do the final floating, brushing away crumbs and smoothing out blemishes with a magnesium hand float *(left)* and a paintbrush. Lightly redo the tooling, if necessary, and float again for a smooth finish. Touch up the surface with a soft brush and cure the concrete.

Adding color

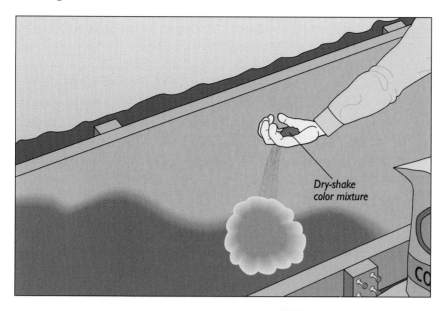

Dry-shake
color mixture

Using a coloring mixture

Dust a dry-shake coloring mixture onto freshly floated concrete, letting the color sift evenly through your fingers. Check the package for how much mixture to use. Color is easier to scatter without gloves, but be sure to wash immediately and apply moisturizing lotion.

Float the surface and apply a second layer of color. Finish the surface with a float, followed by brooming, if desired. After floating, the top $1/8$" to $1/4$" of the concrete will be colored.

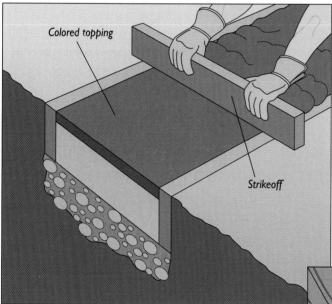

Colored topping

Strikeoff

Placing colored concrete

It's most economical to cast a 1" topping of colored concrete over a plain base. It's best to do so when the concrete is freshly cast. Otherwise, apply a concrete bonding agent to the concrete base before casting the colored concrete on top.

To apply a layer of colored concrete, strike off the base 1" below the top of the forms. Wait for the concrete to firm up and for the surface sheen to disappear. Add pigment to a small batch of cement-sand mix, and place a layer over the fresh slab, striking it off flush *(left)*. Finish and cure as usual. Don't cure colored concrete under a plastic sheet: It will be blotchy.

Using organic concrete stain

First finish the concrete, cure it, and let it dry. Then brush on concrete stain with a 4" paintbrush. Make sure the stain is intended for concrete, and follow the directions on the container. You'll need to reapply the stain periodically.

Stain can be applied to existing concrete slabs, provided they're clean and dry. Old slabs can be cleaned with a solution of laundry detergent or a concrete-cleaning compound and water. Scrub with a wire brush, then flush with clear water.

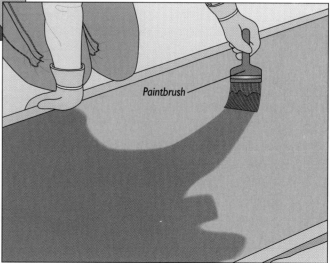

Paintbrush

Building Steps and Walkways

Changes of level in your garden may call for a full flight of steps or perhaps just a stepped walkway that rises gently from level to level.

On these pages we'll show you a few step options, as well as give you basic instructions for building a concrete walkway. Working with concrete on a smaller project like a walkway is easier than casting a large slab *(page 164)*, but you'll still need a few helpers.

Steps: Well-designed steps begin with an understanding of step proportions. The flat surface of a step is called a tread; the vertical surface is a riser. Ideally, the depth of the tread plus twice the riser height should equal 25 to 27 inches. For outdoor steps, a riser height of 6 inches is often recommended, but for very wide stairs, or for stepped walkways, a riser height of about 4½ inches may feel more comfortable. Some good riser-to-tread ratios are illustrated opposite. For stepped walkways, the treads can be longer, two good strides or more usually feels comfortable. To build masonry steps, see page 179.

Walkways: Much more than simply a path on which to move through the yard, a walkway can be an important element in a home landscaping scheme: It divides different activity areas; meandering gently through a heavily planted area, it can entice you out to look at the garden; and it can visually tie disparate elements together. For example, a paved concrete deck around a pool and a raised wooden deck just off the back door can be tied together with a pathway of cast concrete and landscape timbers such as the one shown opposite.

No matter what it's made of—concrete, brick, stone, or a loose material such as wood chips or gravel—a walkway is essentially a long, narrow patio and the steps in building it are the same. You excavate the site down to the required depth (the thickness of the setting bed, whether it's concrete or sand, plus the thickness of the surface material), install edgings to contain the surface material, then place and level the setting bed, and install the surface material on top. For details on installing the various materials, see the appropriate sections earlier in this chapter.

Calculating Step Dimensions

To calculate how many steps you'll need, you first need to know the rise and run of the slope. Place one end of a long, straight 2x4 at the top of the slope where the steps will end and, holding it roughly level, mark the bottom of it where the steps will begin; this is the run. To determine the rise, hold the 2x4 level and measure down from the mark you made to the ground. (Both tasks are easier with a helper.)

Divide the slope's rise by the riser height you want; the result is the number of steps you'll need. If the answer ends in a fraction, drop the fraction and divide the whole number into the rise of the slope to get the exact measurement for each riser.

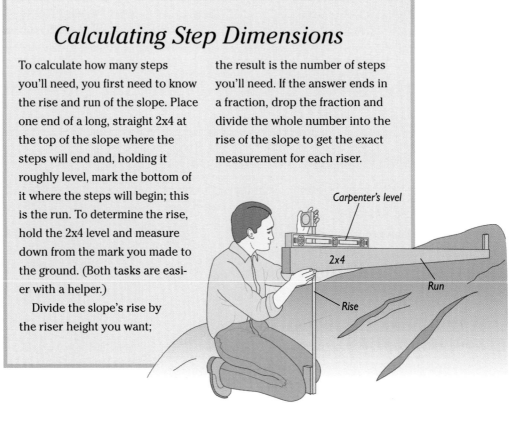

Carpenter's level

2x4

Run

Rise

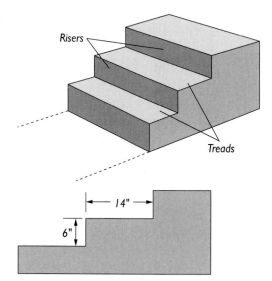

Risers

Treads

14"

6"

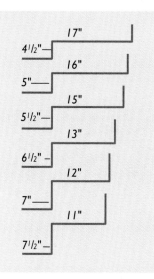

17"
4¹/₂"
16"
5"
15"
5¹/₂"
13"
6¹/₂"
12"
7"
11"
7¹/₂"

STEP PROPORTIONS

Before you can build your own steps, you need to decide on the riser and tread dimensions that are appropriate. As shown at left, the best proportions for steps are achieved when twice the riser height added to the tread depth comes to between 25 and 27 inches. A riser height of 6 inches is common; minimum comfortable tread depth is 11 inches. All risers and treads in any one flight of steps should be uniform in size.

STEP DESIGN OPTIONS

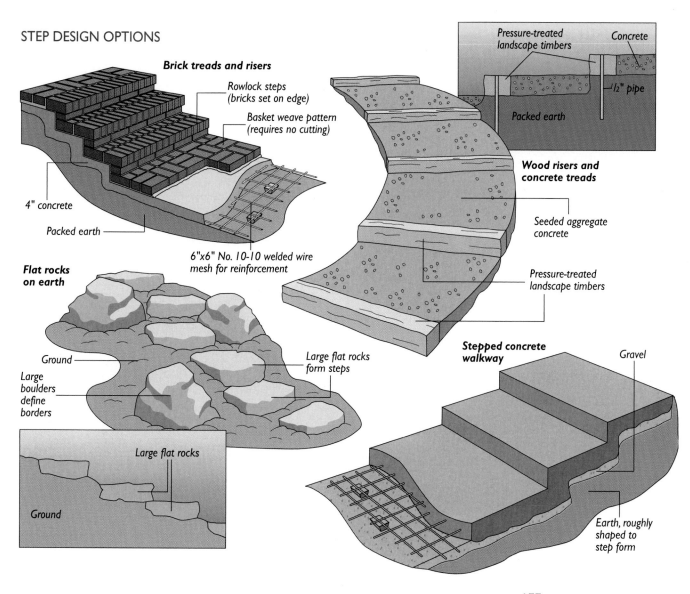

Brick treads and risers

Rowlock steps (bricks set on edge)

Basket weave pattern (requires no cutting)

4" concrete

Packed earth

6"x6" No. 10-10 welded wire mesh for reinforcement

Pressure-treated landscape timbers

Concrete

Packed earth

¹/₂" pipe

Wood risers and concrete treads

Seeded aggregate concrete

Pressure-treated landscape timbers

Flat rocks on earth

Ground

Large boulders define borders

Large flat rocks form steps

Large flat rocks

Ground

Stepped concrete walkway

Gravel

Earth, roughly shaped to step form

Casting a concrete walkway

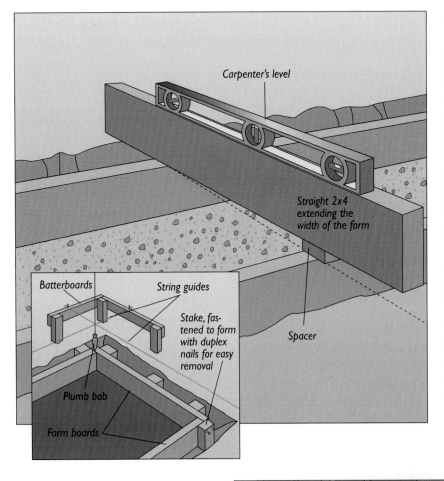

Carpenter's level

Straight 2x4 extending the width of the form

Spacer

Batterboards

String guides

Stake, fastened to form with duplex nails for easy removal

Plumb bob

Form boards

1 Preparing the site

Use batterboards and string to outline your site, making the outline about a foot wider and longer than you need, to allow room for forms. Dig to the required depth. Assemble the forms in the trench, staking them every 4'. Position the corners using string lines attached to batterboards and a plumb bob *(inset)*. Nail and stake the corners. Place and level the gravel base, if you're using one.

To allow water to run off, the concrete should have a pitch of about ¼" per foot. To allow for this, position one form board slightly higher than the other. Check the pitch of the form by placing a level on a long, straight board extending the width of the form; a spacer should be required at one end to level the board *(left)*.

2 Placing the concrete

If you'll be adding masonry units on top of the concrete, use 6" square No. 10-10 welded-wire mesh for reinforcement. Otherwise, add control joints after casting *(page 170)*.

Make sure you have enough helpers and tools, since once you've started placing the concrete, you shouldn't stop until the job is done.

Dampen the soil or gravel and begin placing the concrete at one end of the form, working it up against the form and into corners with a square shovel *(right)*. Shovel the concrete, don't drag it.

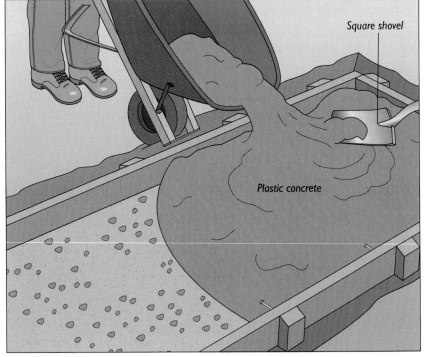

Square shovel

Plastic concrete

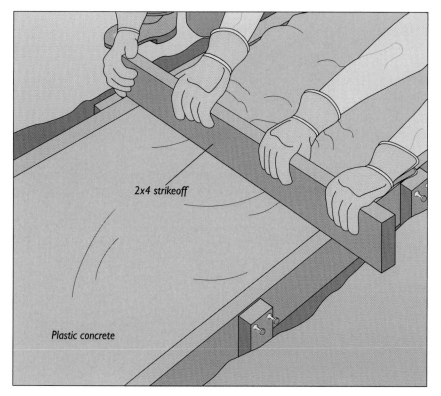

2x4 strikeoff

Plastic concrete

3 Striking and finishing

Once the concrete is placed, strike it off using a straight 2x4; use a bladed strikeoff if you want the finished concrete to be lower than the tops of the forms because you're adding a surface material or colored topping. Move the strikeoff slowly in a zigzagging motion; make two passes. It helps to have two people at this task; a third can shovel concrete into low spots.

Smooth the concrete with a darby, starting with overlapping arcs and making a second pass with straight, overlapping side-to-side strokes.

To finish the concrete, wait until the water sheen has left the surface, then smooth the edges, add control joints, float, and cure the slab as described for a concrete patio on pages 169 to 171.

Building masonry steps

Begin by forming rough steps in the earth, keeping the treads as level and the risers as perpendicular as possible. In nonfreezing climates with granular soil, no gravel is required. Otherwise, be sure to allow for the thickness of a 4- to 6-inch gravel base. Keeping the gravel back from the front of the steps makes the fronts of the treads thicker and therefore stronger. Dig deep enough to accommodate a minimum 4-inch thickness of concrete on both treads and risers and the thickness of masonry units, such as bricks or tiles, if you're planning to add them. (If you're adding masonry units, reinforce with 6"x6" No. 10-10 wire mesh, bending it up the slope from step to step in mid-slab. In severe climates, you may need 6 to 8 inches of concrete.)

Install forms, place and level the gravel if used, then place and strike off the concrete. Broom for a nonslip surface (page 170). Cure the steps (page 171) then install the masonry units, if desired.

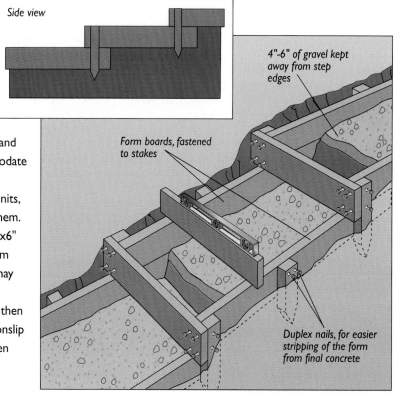

Side view

Form boards, fastened to stakes

4"-6" of gravel kept away from step edges

Duplex nails, for easier stripping of the form from final concrete

Patio
REPAIRS

Patio surface materials, whether individual units like brick or tile, or cast-in-place, such as concrete, are relatively maintenance free. They may require an occasional cleaning, however, and in spite of their durability, they can be damaged. This chapter is your guide to the care and repair of your patio's surface. Generally, you can keep your patio looking great simply by washing it with plain water. For tougher stains, such as oil and grease, refer to the tips on page 182. Shifting earth, impacts, and freeze-thaw cycles can damage even the best-made patios. Patios set in sand may buckle or shift, but repair involves simply removing the offending units, leveling the sand bed beneath them, and replacing them. Repairing mortared units or cast concrete structures is more time-consuming. Instructions for repairing unit masonry include renewing mortar joints (page 183) and replacing an individual unit (page 184). Common repairs for cast concrete include fixing small cracks with grout, patching larger cracks and damaged areas, and repairing step edges; instructions begin on page 185.

Hosing down your patio periodically will control the unsightly buildup of dirt and leaves. Turn to the next page for more information on cleaning patios.

Cleaning Your Patio

Ordinary household detergents and cleaners will handle many stains, but some blemishes, such as mortar smears, will require acid. Specific remedies are given below.

Do not ever use acid on marble or limestone. Clean with water only, as even some harsh detergents can be harmful. Sometimes you can abrade stains on stone by rubbing the stained stone with a piece of the same type of rock.

Use a fiber-bristle brush to scrub masonry; a steel brush is too abrasive and may leave rust marks.

TIPS FOR A PRISTINE PATIO

Efflorescence: Mineral salts brought to the surface by water, which then evaporates, create white, powdery deposits, especially on brick paving. The deposits will disappear after a couple of years, but if you're impatient, try brushing and scrubbing the deposits away without using water, then follow with a thorough hosing. Water tends to redissolve some of the salts, which will reappear again later. For a more lasting treatment, use muriatic acid, following the directions for removing mortar smears, given below.

Oil and grease: Before the stain has penetrated, scatter fine sawdust, cement powder, cat litter, or hydrated lime over the surface. These materials will soak up much of the oil or grease and can be simply swept up. If the stain has penetrated, try dissolving it with a commercial degreaser or emulsifier, available at masonry and home supply centers and at auto suppliers; follow the manufacturer's recommendations. Residual stains can often be lightened with household bleach, as explained for rust. Never use hazardous solvents, such as kerosene, benzene, or gasoline.

Paint: To clean freshly spilled paint, scrub it with a rag soaked in the solvent specified for the paint. For dried paint, use a commercial paint remover, following the manufacturer's instructions.

Rust: Household bleach will lighten rust stains, and most others. Scrub it in, let it stand, and then rinse thoroughly. For a stronger remedy, mix a pound of oxalic acid into a gallon of water; follow the mixing instructions given below for muriatic acid. Brush on the acid, let it stand for three or four minutes, then hose it off. Bleach and acid washes can lighten a surface's color; test an inconspicuous area first.

Removing mortar smears

Use muriatic acid, available at masonry supply stores, to remove mortar smears. It works by attacking the alkalis in concrete and mortar. On light brick, use a 1:14 or 1:19 acid-water solution. Use a 1:9 solution on concrete and dark brick. Don't use acid on colored concrete as it may leach out the color. Never use it on stone. CAUTION: When preparing the solution, always pour the acid slowly into the water—never the reverse. Wear eye protection, rubber gloves, and old clothing, and work in a well-ventilated area.

Working with a small area at a time, first wet it, then apply the acid solution using a stiff nylon brush. Let it stand for three to four minutes, until it stops bubbling, then flush the area thoroughly with water until all the acid has been flushed away.

Repairing Unit Masonry

Most trouble with mortar and paving develops at the mortar joints. Sometimes, mortar will shrink, causing the joints to open. Lime-base mortar, no longer commonly used for paving, may simply crumble.

Freeze-thaw cycles aggravate the problem. Water penetrates the tiniest cracks; when it freezes, it expands, enlarging the cracks and making it more likely that the problem will recur. Renewing the exist-ing mortar joints will eliminate shrinking, crumbling, and cracking.

Settling can crack the joints of a mortared pavement, and sometimes the units themselves will crack. A heavy impact can do the same thing. The remedy is to replace the damaged units and mortar. In extreme cases, you may need to rebuild an entire section of the patio.

The repairs shown here apply to all types of unit masonry paving set in wet mortar, even though not all are shown in the illustrations.

Replacing a damaged stone is tricky. It's difficult to get an individual stone out and to fit a new one into the gap. You will likely have to score and cut the new stone to fit. Replacing evenly sized units is easier. You can reuse an undamaged brick if all old mortar is carefully chiseled off. Clean and soak the brick in water before reinstalling it.

Renewing mortar joints

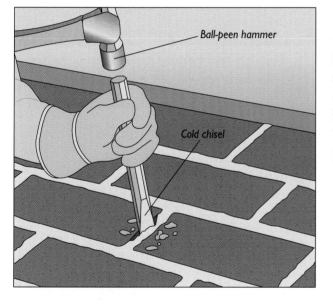

Ball-peen hammer

Cold chisel

1 Chiseling out the joint
Using a narrow-bladed cold chisel and a ball-peen hammer, chisel out the old mortar, exposing as much of the mortar-bearing faces of the units as possible. For bricks and other thick units, expose the joints to a depth of at least ¾"; for units less than ¾" thick, chisel out to the base. Thoroughly brush and blow out the joints, using an old paintbrush. Wear eye protection for this entire task.

2 Adding new mortar
Dampen the area with a fine spray of water or a wet brush. Mix Type S mortar *(page 142)* to a stiff consistency while waiting for the surface moisture to evaporate.

When the units are damp, but not shiny wet, use a joint filler or a small pointing trowel to press mortar into the joints; a hawk will keep mortar handy. Fill the joints completely, tamping the mortar in well (use a small piece of wood for deep joints). Tool the joints when the mortar is stiff enough. Keep the repair damp for three days, to cure the mortar.

New mortar

Pointing trowel

Replacing a unit

1 Removing the damaged unit
Wearing eye protection, chip away the old mortar as described for renewing a mortar joint on page 183. Work carefully so as not to damage adjacent units. Break up the damaged unit with a cold chisel or hand-drilling hammer *(right)*. If you're removing a tile, first score an X across it with a glass cutter. Chip away all the old mortar beneath the unit.

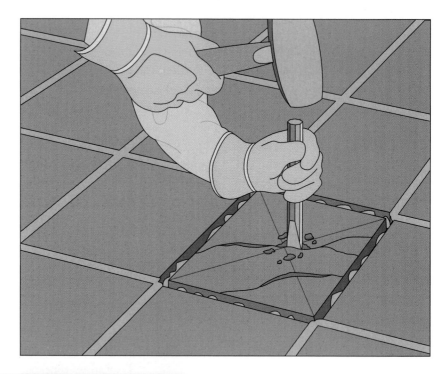

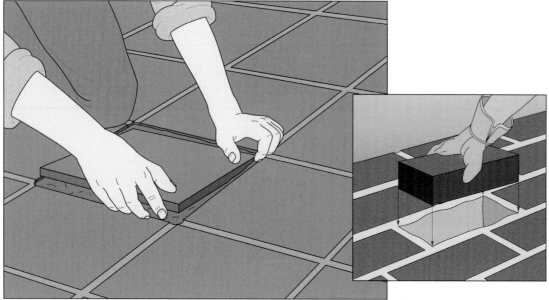

2 Installing the new unit
The installation process is the same for brick and other paving units. Dampen the cavity and the replacement unit with a fine spray of water or a wet brush. Prepare a batch of mortar with a 1:2 cement-sand mix to the consistency of soft mud. If you're using ceramic tile, use a commercially packaged mix, either dry-set portland cement mortar or latex portland cement mortar. Make sure the cavity is damp but not wet, then apply a thick layer of mortar to the bottom and sides of the cavity. Push the new unit into place. Mortar should squeeze from the joints; if not, add more. Trim off excess mortar and tool the joints. Keep the area damp for three days to cure the new mortar. You may need to grout the joints to fill them.

Repairing Cast Concrete

Concrete is hard and durable, but if it's not placed, finished, and cured properly, flaws can develop. Impacts, shifting earth, and freeze-thaw cycles also take their toll.

Dusting, in which the surface powders easily, may be the result of insufficient curing, but it's not a serious problem for an outdoor slab. Scaling, in which thin layers flake away from the surface, may be caused by freeze-thaw cycles or by the use of chemical de-icers. Instructions for dealing with both minor and severe surface problems are given on page 187.

Efflorescence, the appearance of white, powdery mineral salts on the surface of the concrete, is not really a flaw. It tends to occur naturally and will disappear in time. To hurry it along, follow the directions for removing efflorescence given on page 182.

Other than surface repairs, you may need to fill small cracks *(below)* or patch larger ones *(page 186)*. Catching and fixing a problem before it becomes something major will help extend the life of your concrete paving.

The success of any concrete patching job depends on the care you take in preparing the surface. Always clean all dust and debris from the area to be repaired using a scrub brush and a commercial concrete-cleaning solution. The area should be damp but not wet when you apply the patch, to ensure a good bond. Either dampen it with a fine spray of water, or thoroughly soak it and wait until no standing water is left. Soaking it the day before you intend to apply the patch usually works quite well.

In any repair in which the patch will be thin or will need to be feathered at its edges, you'll find the extra strength of commercial latex patching compounds (sold under various trade names) well worth their extra cost.

Filling small cracks

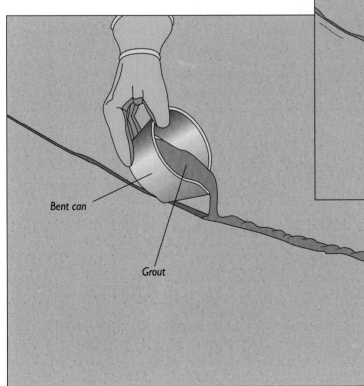

Bent can

Grout

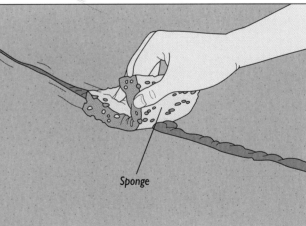

Sponge

A long, open crack is easiest to fix by filling it with grout. Wet the surface the day before, as described above, or dampen it with a wet brush or fine spray. Prepare a 1:2 cement-fine sand mixture that's thin enough to pour. When the surface is damp but not wet, pour the grout into the crack from a bent can *(left)*, then smooth the surface with a damp sponge *(inset)*. A commercial concrete patcher will also work well.

Making a patch

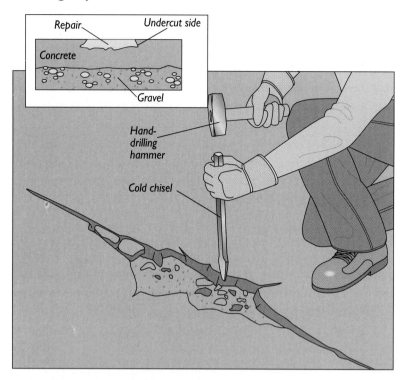

Repair · Undercut side

Concrete

Gravel

Hand-drilling hammer

Cold chisel

1 Chiseling out the crack

Wearing eye protection, use a cold chisel and a hand-drilling hammer to remove loose material and deepen the crack to create a pocket ¾" deep or more *(left)*. Undercut the sides *(inset)* to help lock the patch to the slab, and smooth the edges as much as possible.

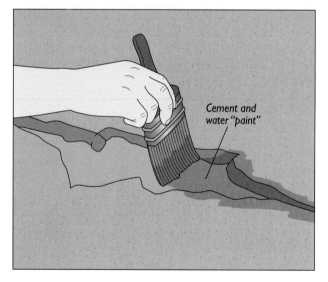

Cement and water "paint"

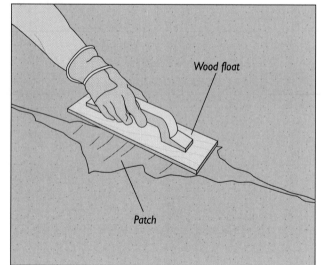

Wood float

Patch

2 Preparing to fill the crack

Clean out the area with a paintbrush dipped in water, removing any bits of concrete that come loose. Either wet the area long enough in advance so that it's only damp when you come to apply the patch, or dampen the crack and surrounding area with a wet brush or a fine spray. To improve the bond of the patch, coat the area with a thick-cream mix of cement and water, the consistency of paint *(above)* or use a latex concrete bonding compound.

3 Finishing the patch

If you've used a cement and water mixture or a latex bonding compound, apply the patch immediately —don't let the coating dry. Using a pointing trowel, fill the crack with a 1:2¼ cement-sand mix with the consistency of soft mud, or a latex patching compound. Finish the patch to match the surrounding surface with a magnesium float or wood float *(above)* and cure for at least three days.

Badly broken concrete slabs or walkways can be rebuilt with more concrete. For the neatest repair, straighten up the edges of the broken area using an abrasive blade in an old circular saw.

If the damage extends to an edge, you'll need to build forms to contain the new concrete, and separate the old from the new with isolation-joint strips *(page 167)*. If the damage is fully contained in the slab, the new concrete should be tied in to the old using rebar. In the area to be repaired, you need to drill holes into the edges of the concrete and fasten pieces of ½-inch rebar in place so they extend over the damaged area. Use 18-inch-long pieces and set them 24 inches on center. You can purchase a kit containing the epoxy you'll need; use a special gun to apply it.

In either case, begin by breaking up the concrete; use a small sledgehammer, and wear safety goggles. If the gravel base has sunk, build it up with more gravel or sand and tamp it well.

Dampen the area, mix a batch of $1:2\frac{1}{4}:2\frac{1}{2}$ cement-sand-aggregate concrete to fill the area, and cast it. Finish the repair to match the surrounding area, and cure it for at least three days.

Dealing with surface flaws

Preventing further damage
Freeze-thaw cycles and the use of de-icing salts can cause scaling. If damage is light, you can help protect the concrete from further deterioration by coating it with a solution of linseed oil and mineral salts.

Clean the area and brush on a 1:1 solution of linseed oil and mineral spirits *(above)*. You'll need to renew this coating every two years or so. It will darken the patio surface.

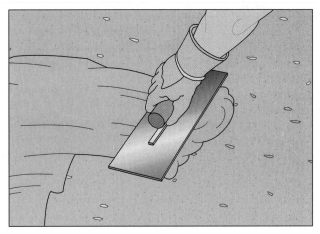

Repairing severe damage
Resurface severely damaged areas with a 1:2¼ portland cement-sand mix or a commercial latex-base resurfacing compound. First remove all loose and flaking concrete with a sledgehammer. Then scrub the area clean and dampen it. Mix a paintlike slurry of portland cement and water; cover only as large an area as you can work before it dries. Before the slurry dries white, trowel on the resurfacing material *(above)*; if you are using a latex-base resurfacing mixture, follow manufacturer's directions. Smooth it with a steel trowel. If you're doing only a small area, feather the edges of the patch; if you're resurfacing the whole slab, use an edger for neat edges. Finish the surface to match existing surfaces and cure for at least three days.

Repairing steps

1 Preparing the site

Repair steps using either a regular cement-sand mix, or a commercial latex patching compound.

If a piece has broken away from a step, simply cement it back in place using an epoxy adhesive intended for outdoor use. If the damage is more extensive, chisel away the concrete until you have an undercut ledge of sound concrete that will support and retain a patch. Wear eye protection when chiseling.

Premixed commercial latex patching compounds are often stiff enough to support themselves—they do not require forms. However, if you use a regular cement-sand mix or are making large repairs, simple temporary formwork is a good idea. This can be nothing more than a board held against the step edge with blocks, as shown. Thoroughly clean and dampen the area to be repaired several hours before placing the patch.

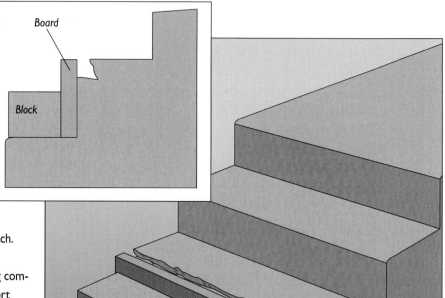

2 Patching

With a paintbrush, brush on a coat of cement and water mixture, the consistency of paint, or a commercial latex-base bonding compound. Follow it immediately with a 1:2¼ cement-sand mix made as dry as possible or a commercial latex patching compound. Thoroughly prod the material with a trowel to eliminate air pockets, then smooth it with a steel trowel. When the patch has stiffened slightly, finish it with an edger *(above)*.

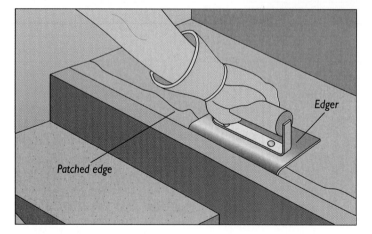

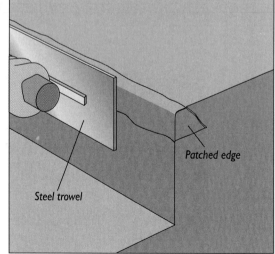

3 Finishing the repair

Carefully remove the form board and use a steel trowel to touch up the face of the step *(above)*. Cover and cure the patch for several days. If you're using a commercial compound, follow the manufacturer's instructions.

Index

Acknowledgments

The editors wish to thank the following:

American Marazzi Tile, Sunnyvale, TX

Bomanite Corporation, Madera, CA

Brick Institute of America, Reston, VA

Country Floors, Montreal, Que.

Endicott Clay Products, Fairbury, NE

Glen-Gery Corporation, Wyomissing, PA

Construction Morival Ltée., Montreal, Que.

National Concrete Masonry Association, Herndon, VA

Portland Cement Association, Skokie, IL

Tile Council of America, Princeton, NJ

Contributing Art Directors:

Jean-Pierre Bourgeois, Michel Giguère

Contributing Illustrators:

Gilles Beauchemin, Jacques Perrault

The following people also assisted in the preparation of this book:

Eric Beaulieu, Lorraine Doré, Pascale Hueber, Valery Pigeon-Dumas, Mathieu Raymond-Beaubien

Picture Credits

6   Jean-Claude Hurni

8   Jean-Claude Hurni

9   (upper) Crandall & Crandall,
     (lower) Philip Harvey

10   (upper) Jean-Claude Hurni,
     (lower) Saxon Holt

11   (upper) Jean-Claude Hurni,
     (lower) Saxon Holt

12   Bill Ross

13   (upper) Richard Nicol,
     (lower) Jean-Claude Hurni

14   (upper) Jean-Claude Hurni,
     (lower) Crandall & Crandall

15   (upper) Peter O. Whiteley,
     (lower) Richard Nicol

16   Stephen Cridland

17   (left) Crandall & Crandall,
     (right) Philip Harvey

18   Jean-Claude Hurni

20   Jean-Claude Hurni

21   Jean-Claude Hurni

22   Jean-Claude Hurni

23   Stephen Cridland

24   Jean-Claude Hurni

25   (upper) Crandall & Crandall,
     (lower) Jean-Claude Hurni

27   Crandall & Crandall

31   Jean-Claude Hurni

34   Jean-Claude Hurni

35   Jean-Claude Hurni

50   Jean-Claude Hurni

54   Robert Chartier

55   Stephen Cridland

58   Tom Wyatt,
     (inset) Richard Nicol

59   Robert Chartier

60   Don Normark

61   (both) Jean-Claude Hurni

63   Robert Chartier

64   Jean-Claude Hurni

65   (left) Jean-Claude Hurni,
     (right) Richard Nicol

66   Robert Chartier

67   Rob Super

68   Robert Chartier

69   Tom Wyatt

70   Tom Wyatt

71   Jean-Claude Hurni

73   Jack McDowell

74   Crandall & Crandall

75   Crandall & Crandall

76   Courtesy Bomanite Corporation

77   Richard Nicol

80   Richard Nicol

82   (left) Richard Nicol,
     (right) Russ Widstrand

83   Crandall & Crandall

84   Jean-Claude Hurni

86   Tom Wyatt

87   Jean-Claude Hurni

92   Philip Harvey

94   (left) Jack McDowell,
     (right) Norman A. Plate

95   Tom Wyatt

96   (both) Jean-Claude Hurni

97   Jean-Claude Hurni (3)

98   (inset) Bill Ross,
     (lower) Crandall & Crandall
        Design: Nick Williams & Assoc.

100 Peter Christiansen

102 Ells Marugg

104 Jean-Claude Hurni

105 Stuart Watson (3)

108 Jean-Claude Hurni

110 Tom Wyatt

111 Crandall & Crandall

112 Stephen Marley

116 Russ Widstrand

117 Jean-Claude Hurni

119 Richard Nicol

120 (left) Jean-Claude Hurni,
     (right) Norman A. Plate

121 Russ Widstrand

123 Crandall & Crandall

180 Jean-Claude Hurni